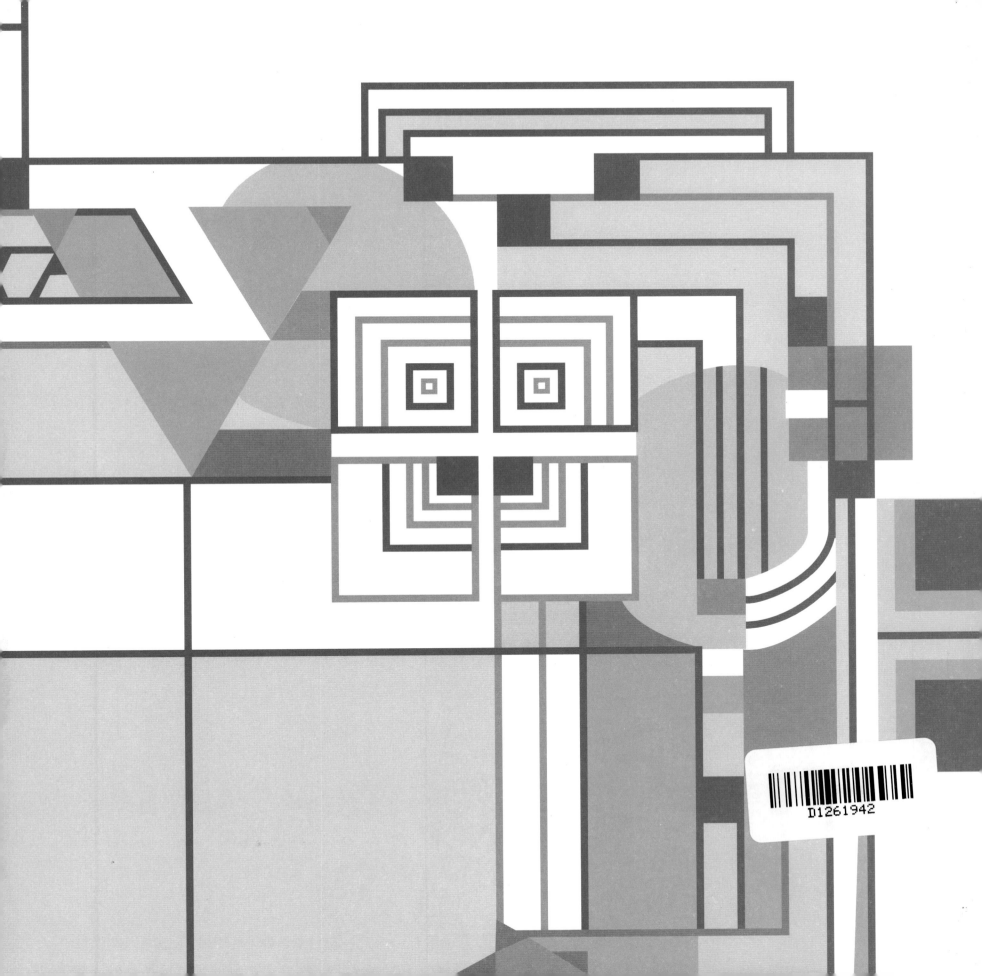

A LIVING ARCHITECTURE

FRANK LLOYD WRIGHT AND TALIESIN® ARCHITECTS

A LIVING ARCHITECTURE

FRANK LLOYD WRIGHT AND TALIESIN. ARCHITECTS

JOHN RATTENBURY

Pomegranate

SAN FRANCISCO

Published by
Pomegranate Communications, Inc.
Box 6099, Rohnert Park, CA 94927
www.pomegranate.com
Pomegranate Europe Ltd.
Fullbridge House, Fullbridge
Maldon, Essex CM9 4LE, England

Catalog No. A571

Library of Congress Cataloging-in-Publication Data

Rattenbury, John.
   A living architecture : Frank Lloyd Wright and Taliesin Architects / JohnRattenbury.
      p.cm.
   ISBN 0-7649-1366-2
   1. Taliesin Architects (Firm) 2. Architecture, Modern--20th century--United States. 3.
Organic architecture--United States. 4. Wright, Frank Lloyd, 1867-1959--Influence. I.
Title.

NA737.T333 R38 2000
720'.92'2--dc21

                                                                              00-037315

ISBN 0-7649-1366-2

Designed by Kimberley Young
Photo editor: Michael French
Produced by Warwick Publishing Inc., Toronto
Printed in Italy

09 08 07 06 05 04 03 02 01 00   10 9 8 7 6 5 4 3 2 1

Page 1: *Monona Terrace—the long awaited wedding between the city and beautiful Lake Monona*

Page 2: *Aztec Lounge at the Arizona Biltmore—a mystical and memorable space.*

Page 4: *The Myers Residence—the ground itself is a basic component of the building.*

ACKNOWLEDGMENTS

Profound thanks to my friends who reassured me that I could write this book. My colleagues at Taliesin—Bruce Brooks Pfeiffer, Margo Stipe, Karen Holden and Bill Mims all gave helpful comments. Others who read the text and made useful suggestions include Mike and Shirley Marty, Tari Wood, Sandy Sims, Ryc Loope, Gerry Jones, Jack Skinner and Eric Lloyd Wright. Research help came from Reed Adamson, Oskar Munoz, Elizabeth Dawsari, Helen Hynes, Elaine Dawson and Dan Bitenc.

Michael French, who shot many of the photographs, also took the time to help us set up an effective archival system to store the thousands of images of our work that we have collected over the years. He and Jim Williamson, the publisher, provided excellent advice and constant encouragement.

I will be eternally grateful to Frank and Olgivanna Lloyd Wright. As my best teachers, they continue to provide inspiration to my work and life at Taliesin. In their own lifetimes, they were generous to me with personal guidance and true friendship.

To the many architects, artists, apprentices, educators and friends at Taliesin whose names are not included or whose designs were left out, my regrets that there was not enough space to recognize your many contributions to Taliesin.

The book is dedicated to Kay, my best friend, wife, and partner in architecture for forty-six wonderful years. Her patience and love overcame every difficulty, her unbounded faith lifted my spirit.

TABLE OF CONTENTS

THE PROJECTS

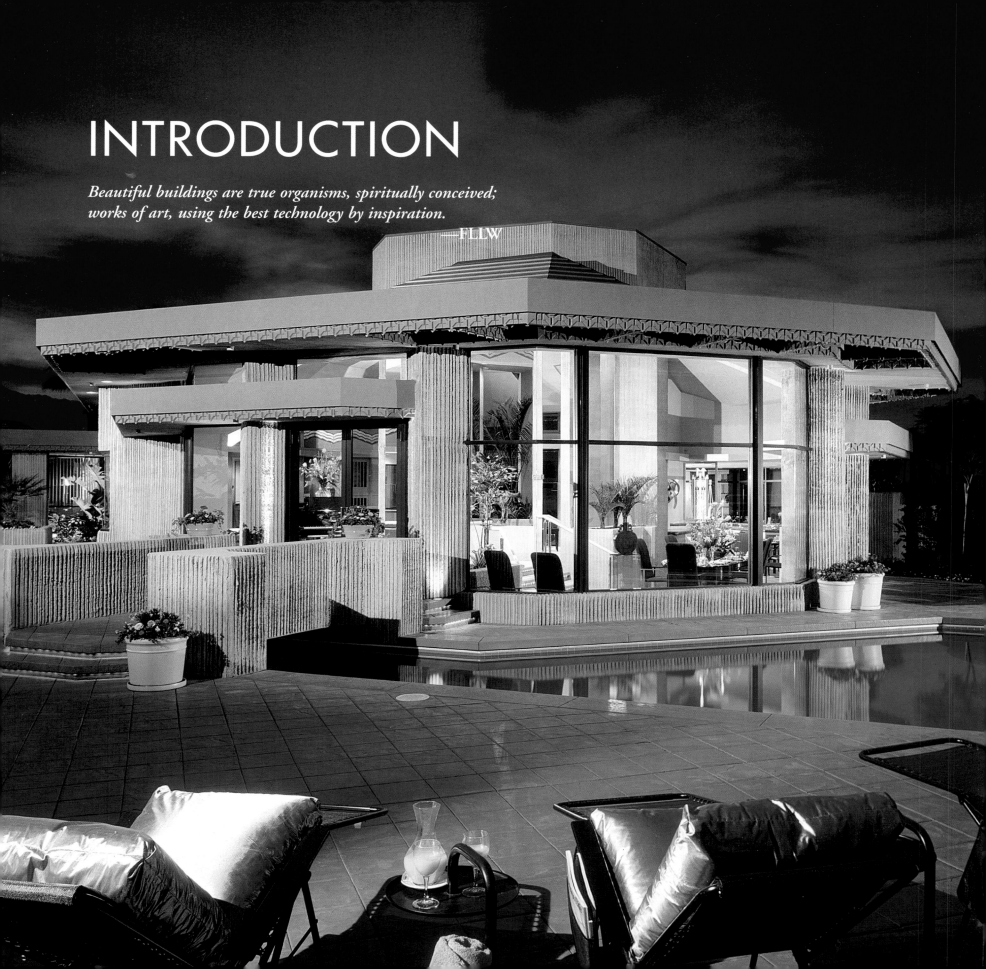

INTRODUCTION

Beautiful buildings are true organisms, spiritually conceived;
works of art, using the best technology by inspiration.

—FLLW

The story of organic architecture is the search for an ideal. It is an exploration by mankind to design and build beautiful structures that serve our needs, make our lives better, and lift our spirits higher. A living architecture will preserve our earthly heritage and give form to the vision of a better future. It will forever be a challenge, a journey that never ends.

Frank Lloyd Wright, heralded by many as the most creative and visionary architect in history, is the father of organic architecture. His work endures in large part because of his timeless ideas, which are inseparable from his architecture. Alive as ever, the power of his ideas and wisdom will long outlive his buildings. They will be his greatest gift to the future, a positive influence for generations ahead.

Despite the growing interest of the public in his work, architecture today, as practiced by the profession and taught in the academic world, has not yet caught up with these ideas, nor realized their true significance. Over two hundred books have been written about Frank Lloyd Wright, but little has been said about the continuation of organic architecture. He urged architects not to copy his work, but to design their own forms according to principles. He never wanted organic architecture to become a style, but to be a great idea that would continue to evolve. To ensure that this would happen he left another legacy beyond his buildings—an architectural firm and a school of architecture.

Leading this effort to advance organic architecture is the firm of Taliesin Architects, the continuation of the studio that Wright started. Together with the Frank Lloyd Wright School of Architecture and the Taliesin

Left: *Sunstream, Desert Springs, California—redefining the American home.*

Below: *The Myers Residence, Scottsdale, Arizona—inspiration for the design came from nature's sculpture, giant boulders strewn over the site.*

Fellowship, it carries on a search for ways in which architecture can make our world a better place to live in.

In 1932, Wright and his wife, Olgivanna, created the Taliesin Fellowship, a group of young apprentices who came from all over the world. An extension of his architectural practice, it was an educational endeavor based on experiential learning. After Wright died in 1959, many of those who were studying and working with him stayed on to form Taliesin Architects. At Taliesin (pronounced *Tally essin*), architecture is a way of life that embraces the concept of life-long learning. The wide range of activities and interests of the group creates a climate that nurtures the creative spirit. Over the past sixty-five years, more than one thousand young men and women have lived, studied and worked at Taliesin. These resident apprentices come to learn organic architecture in depth—by participating in projects in the studio, engaging in construction, and sharing in community life and culture.

What is our motivation, our passion? To build buildings that are beautiful and in harmony with nature. To design architecture that inspires people to become better human beings. To make a contribution to the future of civilization.

In a span of four decades, Taliesin Architects has designed over 1,300 projects worldwide. The representative projects in this book demonstrate the breadth of the work and confirm that adherence to principle does not limit the creative ability of an architect.

Organic architecture may be better understood by identifying its essential qualities and observing how an infinite variety of forms can spring from simple and elemental ideas.

Three objectives form the mainstream of this book:

- To explore and define the philosophy and principles that underlie organic architecture, explain why they endure, and illustrate how they may be applied.

- To encourage public appreciation of the qualities that organic architecture contributes to our lives and our environment.

- To share with the world a vision of how a living architecture can improve life in the future.

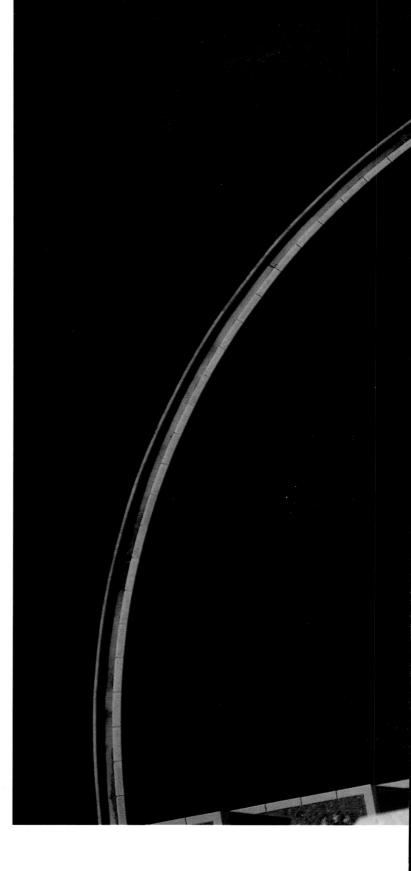

FRANK LLOYD WRIGHT

Is it not interesting that Frank Lloyd Wright is an inexhaustible vein of the purest ore? There is not the slightest sign that his fascination is waning.

—Grant Carpenter Manson

Frank Lloyd Wright was a man in the right place, at the right time. Before he was born in 1867, his mother decided he would become an architect. There is an old proverb: "Destiny is not a matter of chance; it is a matter of choice. It is not a thing to be waited for; it is a thing to be achieved." During his childhood his mother imbued in Wright a love of nature, a love that became the greatest inspirational force in his life. Nature became his bible. "We spell God with a capital G," he said, " and I spell Nature with a capital N."

Far left: *Frank Lloyd Wright with Wes Peters, Jack Howe and Gene Masselink.*

Frank Lloyd Wright with apprentices—he inspired the youth of the world.

followed traditional styles and designed according to specific formulas. The classical forms they followed were imported from Europe; Wright believed the United States should have an architecture of its own, and he set out to create it. As the defining force of organic architecture, he has added immeasurably to the quality of our lives. He did not, however, claim to invent organic architecture. He found it manifested everywhere in nature. He found evidence of architecture true to its time and place in the ancient cultures of Persia, Byzantium, China, Japan, and Pre-Columbian America.

The principles and tenets that he articulated are evidence of his constant search for universal truth. Even his earliest work had about it the countenance of principle, and as his work continued to evolve one can see both ideals and ideas at work. Wright saw architecture as a great source of inspiration to mankind and was convinced that it must constantly evolve and respond to new technology. He believed that architecture would be our contribution to the great civilizations of the future.

He was convinced that lifelong learning is essential. In an ideal society, the teachers, he observed, would be those who had achieved the highest level of human development and had accomplished something worthwhile in life. But he found most learning institutions to be theoretical and dogmatic. He did not believe that the essentials of life could be taught in a classroom—they have to be experienced. Education without enlightenment, he concluded, is merely a matter of conditioning, a drift towards conformity. Wright looked for the day when those involved in art, science

His career started in Chicago, where there were many opportunities for building following the great fire of 1871. His innovative ideas for structure were made possible by the availability of many new materials and construction methods—steel, sheet metal, reinforced concrete, plate glass, and plastics. At the root of Wright's genius was his amazing ability for absorption. He saw everything in life as something to be looked into, something to learn from. Although Nature was his most significant teacher, he had many other influences in his life. Largely self-educated, he was an avid reader. Among his many heroes were Thomas Jefferson, Ralph Waldo Emerson, Bach, Beethoven, William Blake, Lao-tse, Leonardo da Vinci, Hokusai, Hiroshige, Walt Whitman, and Louis Sullivan.

He opened his first architectural office in Chicago in 1893. As his ideas and designs evolved, Wright began to articulate a philosophy of what he termed "organic architecture." At the time he entered the profession, virtually all architects in the Western world and religion realized that their interest and source of inspiration are one and the same.

Twenty years after his death, *Architectural Record* polled the world's leading architects and scholars to determine the hundred most significant buildings in the world in the past hundred years. Twelve of those selected were by Frank Lloyd Wright. Fallingwater was at the top of the list and six of his designs placed in the top twenty-five.

In 1949 he was awarded the AIA Gold Medal, the highest honor of The American Institute of Architects. The citation read:

■ *Prometheus brought fire from Olympus and endured the wrath of Zeus for his daring; but his torch lit other fires and man lived more fully by their warmth. To see the beacon fires he has kindled is the greatest reward for one who has stolen fire from the gods.*

■ *Frank Lloyd Wright has moved men's minds. People from all over the world believe in the inherent beauty of architecture which grows from need, from the soil, from the nature of materials. He is a titanic force in making them so believe.*

■ *Frank Lloyd Wright has built buildings. Structure, in his hands, has thrown off stylistic fetters and taken its proper place as the dominant guiding force in the solution of man's creative physical problems.*

■ *Frank Lloyd Wright has kindled men's hearts. An eager generation of architects stands today as his living monument. By precept and example he has imparted to them the courage to live an architectural ideal. They are reaching leadership in our profession, themselves dedicated to creating order and beauty, not as imitators, but as servants of truth.*

■ *It is for that courage, that flame, that high-hearted hope, that contribution to the advancement of architectural thought that this Gold Medal, the highest award of The American Institute of Architects, is presented to Frank Lloyd Wright.*

Olgivanna Lloyd Wright—the only art that endures is that which carries a universal meaning.

TALIESIN AND THE TALIESIN FELLOWSHIP

There is no quest, no search possible to human endeavor that is not connected with and in some way producing that which is beautiful.
—FLLW

Near Spring Green, Wisconsin, alongside the Wisconsin River, lies the lovely and verdant Lloyd Jones Valley. It was here that Frank Lloyd Wright worked as a young boy on his uncle James's farm, developing a work ethic and learning from nature. And it was here that his aunts, Ellen and Jane Lloyd Jones, founded the Hillside Home School in 1886. It was the first coeducational boarding school in the country, and its design was Wright's first architectural commission. Dedicated to the concept of experiential learning, the school was a radical departure from the educational practices of the time, a noble experiment that lasted until 1915.

When Wright decided to build his home in this valley, he called it Taliesin, a Welsh word meaning "Shining Brow." Taliesin wraps around the brow of the hill; it is of the hill and not on it. Wright spent forty-eight years building and expanding Taliesin, rebuilding it twice after fires destroyed the living quarters. It has been called by many the most beautiful house in the world.

In 1924, while attending a performance of the Russian Ballet at Orchestra Hall in Chicago, Wright met Olgivanna Lazovich Hinzenburg. She would become his wife for the next thirty-five years. Olgivanna's views on art, philosophy, and education were similar to his. Born in Montenegro and educated in Russia, she later studied at the Institute for the Harmonious Development of Man, under a remarkable teacher, G. I. Gurdjieff. Gurdjieff's philosophy embraced the integrated development of mind, heart, body, and spirit through experiential learning.

Taliesin West—where architecture is a way of life.

Wright's experience with the Hillside Home School and Olgivanna's training with Gurdjieff gave them a similar approach to education.

At this time, around the onset of the Great Depression, there was little architectural work in the country. In 1928, Olgivanna said to her husband, "You have built many buildings and many more will come. Why not build people—build architects. Educate young men and women in the philosophy and principles of organic architecture. They could learn by helping you with your work."

Wright, who absorbed ideas as readily as a person breathes, picked up the thought and immediately started planning. "No drafting board architects for us, they must get their hands into construction, learn the nature of materials; learn from the bottom up, not the top down. They can fix up the buildings at Taliesin and Hillside that need repair. They will have a complete life, participate in all the allied arts."

They began developing the idea of a school for architects and artists. Deciding to call it the Hillside Home School for the Allied Arts, they invited a friend, the Dutch architect Th. Wijdeveld, who had previously published Wright's work, to join them in establishing and running it. After seeing the sad condition of the long-deserted buildings of the former school, Wijdeveld declared the idea unfeasible. Unable to acquire funding, the Wrights abandoned the idea.

Yet the thought of some sort of educational program remained constant in their minds. In 1932, with a great deal of courage but very little money, they went ahead with their plan, not on such a broad scope as originally planned, but more focused on architecture. This was the birth of the Taliesin Fellowship, a unique educational idea based on experiential learning.

Apprentices came from all over the world to work with Wright in his studio. The Fellowship produced the construction drawings for Fallingwater, the Johnson Wax Administration Building, the Guggenheim Museum and over four hundred more of his designs. Over half of these designs were constructed. The Fellowship also rebuilt and expanded the buildings at Taliesin and Hillside, adding a new studio. In 1937, they started building Taliesin West, a winter campus in the Arizona desert. The Taliesin Fellowship was largely a self-sufficient community and, during the years of the Second World War, operated the Taliesin farm and grew its own food. In addition to work in the studio, construction and the farm, Fellowship life included cooking, shopping, cleaning, landscaping, cultural and social activities. Everything was related to architecture, and architecture became a way of life.

There is insufficient space to include the names of all the Taliesin Fellows, now over a thousand, but three stand out. They were known as Wes, Jack, and Gene. All three were charter members, joining the Fellowship in 1932 or shortly thereafter, and each made a unique and lasting contribution.

William Wesley Peters was both an architect and an engineer. Working with Mendel Glickman, a former apprentice, he did the structural engineering for almost every building that Wright designed after 1932. Wes was able to combine his engineering ability with a remarkably creative design talent, and after Taliesin Architects was formed, he designed many of the firm's major buildings until his death in 1991.

While Mr. Wright was alive, the members of the Fellowship were all, to some extent, pencils in his hand. None could compare with John Henry Howe, known as Jack. In the morning, Mr. Wright would sit at his drafting board and in clear, bold lines sketch

Teamwork—the spirit of independence, instinct, and cooperation.

out the plan, section, and elevations for a design concept. Not until he had the idea clearly articulated in his mind, in three dimensions, did he commit it to paper. Jack would take his sketches and with lightning speed turn them into presentation drawings. He could lay out a two-point perspective so fast that it seemed his pencil must catch on fire.

Gene Masselink served as Mr. Wright's business manager. He was also a fine artist. As he absorbed the principles of organic architecture he became fascinated by the nature patterns that inspired Wright's work. Gene created beautiful abstractions, murals, and graphic designs. A warm, kind and gentle soul with a fine sense of humor, he had the knack of uplifting everyone's spirits.

Taliesin attracts fine people and, given the chance, it brings out the best in them. These three, and many other Taliesin Fellows, are no longer alive, but their work lives on.

In 1940 Wright established the Frank Lloyd Wright Foundation as the repository of his life's work. When he died in 1959, twenty-six years after starting the Taliesin Fellowship, Olgivanna assumed the lead-

Learning construction skills through hands-on experience.

ership role. For the next twenty-five years, under her inspired guidance, the Fellowship flourished. Few people are aware of her role in Taliesin Architects. She reviewed every design that came out of the office, gave constructive critiques, ideas, and encouragement. She was also our color consultant, a role that she played in her husband's practice.

Mrs. Wright made a significant contribution to the Fellowship in another manner—she thought of many ways to nurture the creative spirit of all the artists and architects. For three summers, she took the entire Fellowship to Europe. The firm opened an office in

Switzerland, and in this different world, was exposed to other cultures firsthand.

She also encouraged the Fellowship to participate in the performing arts—music, dance, and drama. Iovanna Lloyd Wright choreographed and wrote productions for the annual Taliesin Festival of Music and Dance, while Mrs. Wright wrote the music. Fellowship members acted, danced, and designed and made the costumes and scenery, and arranged the theatrical lighting. Performances were given in our own theater in Arizona, and also Wisconsin, Chicago, San Francisco, and Dallas. The experience gave us a profound understanding of theater design as well as energizing everyone and expanding our artistic spirit.

Mrs. Wright played an important role in the firm, supporting its public relations by giving lectures around the country and overseas, writing a weekly column for newspapers in Wisconsin and Arizona, and hosting weekly social events at Taliesin. She steered the Fellowship through the difficult transition from a group with a single, charismatic leader to a partnership of many individuals working together as a team.

The spirit of Taliesin Architects may be described as one of independence blended with instinctive cooperation. A principal architect has individual design responsibility for a project, and is supported by the combined resources of the firm—skills, energy and experience. Colleagues offer ideas and comments, but the design is the work of an individual. During the complex effort of taking a project all the way from an idea to a completed building, they work as an interdependent team.

The word Taliesin is the name of Wright's house in Wisconsin, but it is frequently used to refer to all of the endeavors—the Foundation, the school, the archives, and the architectural firm. Forty years after Frank Lloyd Wright died and fourteen years after the loss of Mrs. Wright, Taliesin continues to flourish as several entities:

The Frank Lloyd Wright Foundation is a not-for-

profit institution. It owns and manages two National Historic Landmark properties (Taliesin and Taliesin West), the Frank Lloyd Wright Archives, and the Frank Lloyd Wright School of Architecture. Both Taliesin and Taliesin West are open to the public for educational tours and seminars, hosting over 100,000 visitors a year.

Taliesin Architects is a wholly owned, for-profit subsidiary of the Foundation. With a staff of over fifty that includes fifteen registered architects, its work is found in forty-one states and a number of foreign countries. Headquarters are at Taliesin West in Scottsdale, Arizona, with offices in Spring Green and Madison, Wisconsin. Professional services include architecture, planning, interior design, landscaping, and graphic design.

The Frank Lloyd Wright Archives is the Foundation's greatest treasure. Located at Taliesin West, it is an international resource for museums, architects, businesses, and scholars. Under the leader-

Architects should not be allowed to design a kitchen unless they know how to cook.

ship of Bruce Brooks Pfeiffer, who came to Taliesin as an apprentice in 1949, the Archives produces exhibitions, publications, lectures, films, videos, and reproductions of Wright-designed items. It has published more than forty books on Wright. Considered to be the world's most complete collection of work by an individual artist housed in a single facility, the Archives cares for 22,000 original Wright drawings and 400,000 other archival items—correspondence, manuscripts, and art collections.

The Frank Lloyd Wright School of Architecture is, you might say, the dynamo of Taliesin. The energy it produces, by way of a constant influx of young, inquiring minds, keeps the group vital and growing. Every aspect of life at Taliesin supports a total and integrated learning environment. The school aims to produce architects who are not only highly skilled

but who are responsible, creative, and cultivated human beings.

It still employs the "learning by doing" approach to education that has changed little since the early days of the Fellowship. It offers apprentices a broad education and prepares them to enter the profession of architecture. The program includes work in the architectural studio, with architects serving as mentors. Apprentices gain hands-on experience in construction and also participate in the community work of the Fellowship. Immersing apprentices in the experience of architecture results in a high level of enthusiasm for learning. Apprentices are encouraged to take on responsibility. As they prove their worth, their responsibility is increased.

"The danger of our nation's educational system," said Mrs. Wright, "lies in its surface approach to everything. Instead of going towards the root of the human being, it is leading us further and further away from the root. Why should not educators who have had experience in life inspire the young, imbue them with the idea that the material to develop is the creativity of the human psyche and intellect? Our youth should be reassured that the world does not entirely revolve on an axis of money and power. I think of the human mind as inspired and inspiring, so creative that no machine can touch it."

The Bachelor of Architectural Studies degree is academically accredited, and the Master of Architecture degree has professional accreditation from the National Architectural Accrediting Board. Degrees are but steps along a path of lifelong learning. Wright was ninety years old when someone asked him who was the best student at Taliesin. He replied, "I am going to have to give that honor to . . . myself!"

The Taliesin Fellowship includes the architects, interns, apprentices, faculty, administrators, and support staff of the Taliesin community who live and work together. Each person is involved in several of the many activities: the architectural firm, the educational program, the tour program, fine arts, the archives and library, construction, and landscaping. The group shares the responsibilities for cooking, housekeeping, and social activities.

Like America, Taliesin is a melting pot. New apprentices come from all over the world: the United States, Canada, Mexico, Central and South America; France, Germany, the United Kingdom, Italy, Greece, Bulgaria, Yugoslavia, Egypt, and Israel; Japan, China, Thailand, Korea, and India. With a constant infusion of youth and a cosmopolitan composition, life is never dull. The intermix of age, gender, nationality, religion, and culture provides a dynamic exchange of philosophy and ideas. Self-reliance and instinctive cooperation are embedded in our way of life at Taliesin.

As organic architects, we perform a balancing act—reaching to the sky for an ideal while serving the pragmatic needs of the world. While our heads are in the sky, our feet are firmly planted on the ground.

After sixty-five years, Taliesin is still a flourishing endeavor. Our passion for life and our enthusiasm for creative work follow the essential patterns as established by the Wrights in 1932. Recognizing that change is an inevitable and an essential aspect of life, Taliesin changes and evolves as the times change. The principles on which it is founded, however, remain constant.

If I do nothing more than awaken young minds to the possibilities of architecture as the great element of life, then I will have done all I expected to do.
—FLLW

ORGANIC ARCHITECTURE

Nothing in the world is so powerful as an idea. A good idea never dies and never ceases changing its form of life.
—FLLW

Benton Residence — a house is more a home by being a work of art.

This quotation goes to the heart of an understanding of organic architecture, which is, simply put, an intrinsic, natural, living architecture based on ideas. While following timeless principles, its forms are constantly evolving in response to changing circumstances.

The physical evidence of what a civilization leaves behind resides, to a large extent, in its architecture. In past centuries, architecture in the Western world was a matter of historic styles, fashions contrived by people for a particular period of history, in vogue for a time. When architects could not come up with a new style, they revived or spruced up an old one. In this century, architecture has gone through many styles—International, Modernist, Postmodern, High-tech Modern, Rationalist, Decorative Classic, Deconstructivist, Neoclassic, and yet others.

Wright advised us, "*Style* is important. *A* style is not. Architectural design should never be related to any period, should never be had by pursuing the Greek, Persian, Chinese or Japanese. We have to go, just as they did, to the source. You cannot restate any of the great forms and ideas which have characterized human civilizations. It is impossible if you wish to be a really creative artist. You must, from your own observation, from your own sense of what is right and beautiful, good and true, make your own statement. You cannot get it from books, you cannot get it from some other statement made by someone else except as the significance and the quality of that thing reaches you and inspires you to emulate. There is no substitute for patience, fidelity, and love of the thing—you cannot put your head in place of your heart."

The word "organic" is distinct from "modern." Modern means something "in the mode," or "in style today." Consequently, what is modern today will go out of style tomorrow. Organic architecture, like nature, implies growth and vitality. Since its philosophy reaches far beyond any characteristic forms that would characterize a style, defining it is not easy. Let's be clear about it, there is no prescription. Matters that are profound defy simple and complete definitions. Nobody has easy or finite explanations of the universe, nature, life, or even our own being, so we continue to explore and try to understand these complex and ineffable matters, and in the process, learn new things about them.

As we read a lovely poem, listen to beautiful music, admire a work of art, enjoy a sunset or smell a rose, we discern that appreciation of their beauty is a matter of the heart as much as the head. It is the same with the beauty of architecture. Because architecture is practical and utilitarian, we might expect it to be susceptible of a scientific definition. This expectation is unfortunate where organic architecture is concerned, because its emotional and spiritual content are an essential part of its constitution. Its magic can be appreciated but may vanish when dissected.

To truly appreciate architecture, one must experience it—walk around a building, move through it and spend time in it. Organic architecture will forever defy being cast into a formula, but here is a good summation by Bruce Brooks Pfeiffer:

■ Organic architecture is architecture appropriate to time, appropriate to place, and appropriate to man.

■ Appropriate to time means a building that belongs to the era in which it is created, addresses contemporary life-styles, social patterns and conditions, and employs available materials and new technological methods resourcefully and honestly.

■ Appropriate to place means a building in harmony with its natural environment—a building that in its proportions, materials and design, belongs to its site.

■ Appropriate to man means a humane architecture, in human scale.

What defines architecture as organic? How does an architect approach a design problem from an organic point of view?

The process is a natural one. It proceeds from generals to particulars and is guided by principles. It begins by gathering information and gaining a complete understanding of all aspects of the problem. The solution to the problem lies within the problem itself, and only through a deep and comprehensive understanding of the issue, applied with common sense, will an appropriate design solution be achieved.

The process of creating an appropriate design is not a linear one, where each factor is considered in turn, but one of amalgamation. The simultaneous comprehension of many factors, sorted by priority, leads to the appropriate solution. It is a matter of networking and parallel processing. Along the way, alternative ideas are considered and evaluated. As the idea germinates, the best solution emerges. Keeping a design simple is essential but it is often the hardest step. It means refraining from putting too many ideas into one design. One idea will be enough if it is a

Annunciation Greek Orthodox Church—connecting us to our spirit and our faith.

28

Gammage Auditorium—its design transforms space and transcends time.

good one. A wise person recognizes when they have a bad idea and is willing to throw it out and start afresh. This act takes some courage.

There are many messages for an architect who listens. All must be respected, heard, analyzed, and synthesized. A design must respond to the client's requirements. The budget, schedule, building codes, technology, and other considerations all impose limitations. The site will have its own story to tell.

In most architectural firms we find those who have aesthetic skills, others whose forte is technology, and yet others who handle business. I believe that if a designer has some skill in all three areas it goes a long way towards getting the design right in the first place. Designs that are later changed to accommodate a forgotten essential ingredient often lose contact with the original idea. When a design must be reshaped for this reason, its integrity is compromised.

As technology advances, the process becomes more and more complicated. Often the list of consultants grows to a dozen or more, and the architect is placed in a role similar to the conductor of a symphony orchestra.

As the various conditions of the problem are recognized and opportunities are identified, the procedure itself, ignited by the enthusiasm of the designer, feeds on inspiration and ideas. As is often the case in a creative act, the rule of one-tenth inspiration and nine-tenths perspiration applies. Although the design process follows an organized and scientific procedure, using mundane facts and figures, it has about it an almost mystical aspect. To create something from ideas and inanimate materials, a thing of beauty that touches the human spirit, is surely an act of magic.

I know that architecture is life; or at least it is life itself taking form and therefore the truest record of life as it was lived in the world yesterday, as it is lived today or ever will be lived.

—FLLW

THE PRINCIPLES AND QUALITIES OF ORGANIC ARCHITECTURE

Organic architecture, as Wright envisioned it, embraces a philosophy that embodies certain fundamental principles. As we look not just *at* nature, but *into* it, we find that behind each and every design there are principles at work. Although these principles have an immutable quality, the ways in which they may be expressed through architectural forms is subject to endless variety. "A principle," said Wright, "is a marvelous thing. It never changes. It is elemen-

Lincoln Tower—architecture appropriate to time, place and man.

*Waikapu Valley Country Club — organic
architecture is based on principle, not precedent.*

tal. You first apprehend the nature of the principle, then you begin to realize the limitations, the felicities and the force of the principle."

There is a clear distinction between regulations and principles. Regulations follow formulas. They are controls, rules, prescriptions for action. They change from place to place and over time. Principles are much broader. They are inherent and fundamental truths that spring from the essential nature of a thing. Although it is in the nature of a principle to be absolute, its application can never be absolute. On the contrary, application without diversity is the death of principle.

To take an example from nature, plants follow certain principles in their design. Their structure has integrity, from the roots that anchor the plant to the ground and gather moisture and nutrients from the soil, to the stems that extend into the air bringing leaves and blooms into sunlight. Their design is in harmony with their particular environment, adapted to the specific climate and soil conditions. The countless variations in the ways that principles may be expressed give us the daffodil, the rose, and the chrysanthemum, each delightfully different. Their beauty is inseparable from their function and their form. The patterns of nature are an architect's greatest source of inspiration, not to be copied, perhaps not to even be interpreted, but to be used as a great teacher.

Architecture based on principles constantly evolves and searches for fresh forms. When our designs are based on inspiration and ideas, they are fresh, not copies of something else. We respond to the special and unique circumstances of each new project, embracing the advance of technology and seeking new forms. We continue to explore the principles that connect architecture with nature, with humanity, and with ethical values and spirituality, to search for fundamental ways to design harmonious and inspirational space for human occupation.

San Jose Community Theater—all creation is a matter of principles at work on natural design.

INSPIRATION AND IDEAS

A good idea never dies and never ceases changing its form of life. The creative faculty in us is that quality of getting born into whatever we do, and getting born again and again with fresh patterns as new problems arise. Inspiration is a prayer, a deep-felt wish.

—FLLW

The first principle of organic architecture is that it must be based on ideas—not on formulas, styles, or theories. This is in contradiction to the way it was, and often still is, taught in the academic world. Yet if we analyze the most beautiful, the most functional, the most significant things in nature and in life, we will invariably see that behind each great design there is a great idea at work. In all creative acts, we use our head, listen to our heart, and go with our instinct. When intelligence, feeling, and insight work in harmony, the result far exceeds the sum of the parts.

Wright believed that nothing in the world is so powerful as an idea. Ideas are magic—where do they come from? Inspiration for an idea can come from many sources: from people, from events or works of art. For architecture, there is no better creative source than nature, where we find an infinite number of wonderful forms and patterns.

How can an idea, so ephemeral in its nature, be transformed into the three-dimensional reality of architecture? Nature shows us how. Behind every design in nature there is an underlying discipline of geometry. We see this in the structural formation of rocks (quite obvious in crystals), in the pattern of leaves and petals, in snowflakes. Under a microscope, we find wonderful geometric patterns in the cellular composition of plants and all living organisms, every living creature. Yet never does the consistency of a mathematical discipline prevent variety or diversity. Everything has its own individuality, yet everything works together in the grand scheme of things.

The natural way to apply geometry to architecture is through a unit system, a modular grid. The unit

Right: *Nautilus shell—the integration of shape and structure.*

Below: *Guggenheim Museum—structure and form inseparable.*

system is not a new idea; it was taught at the Ecole de Beaux Arts for years. Many artists have used it in their work. The plan of the traditional Japanese house is based on units three feet by six feet, the size of a *tatami*, or sleeping mat. In organic design, the unit system is a fundamental method of organization. In an architectural plan, the two-dimensional unit, or module, is a square, rectangle, triangle, hexagon, circle, or a mixture of these. Extending the unit system into the third dimension we have a cube, pyramid, sphere, and all the endless variety of shapes that can be achieved by combining them. Throughout the amazing variety of architectural forms that are conceivable, the mathematical, three-dimensional unit system is the essential underlying factor that gives discipline to

Above: *Giant Saguaro cactus—nature is an architect's greatest teacher.*

Right: *The Focus House at Taliesin Gates— blending with the textures of the desert.*

Despite their countless numbers, no two snowflake designs are alike.

Below: *The Snowflake Motel—the growth in space of an idea.*

imagination. We may appreciate the marvelous exuberance of nature, but if we look beneath the surface, we always find discipline.

Although discipline imposes certain limitations on the design process, its boundaries are really good friends to our imagination, keeping it focused, organized, and challenged.

There will always be an element of mystery about the creative act — the birth of the universe, the breath of life, a work of art. As we ponder the imponderable, the words of William Blake come to mind: To see a world in a grain of sand / And a heaven in a wild flower, / Hold infinity in the palm of your hand / And eternity in an hour.

INTEGRITY AND UNITY

What is needed most in architecture is the very thing that is needed most in life, integrity. Just as it is in a human being, so integrity is the deepest quality in a building.

—FLLW

In an organic building, integrity underlies, guides, and coordinates all the other principles. When a design is true to an idea, uncompromising in its effort to harmonize with its physical, social, and cultural environment, and honest in its expression of structure and its use of materials, it has integrity.

One of the basic premises of organic architecture is that the part is to the whole as the whole is to the part. This is its integrity, the same quality that is intrinsic to nature. What is the integrity of a tree, for example? Its purpose, its structure, its form—all are shaped and adapted to the forces of nature. The structural system of roots, trunk, limbs, and twigs are all related to one another, and to the efflorescence of buds and flowers. The size and proportion of each to the other are in balance—color, texture, scent, as well as the system of nourishment and growth. Photosynthesis, absorption of nutrients from the soil, the flow of sap, the storage

36

of energy in the cells, the adjustment to different seasons—all these aspects relate to the whole to form a beautiful and perfect organic entity.

Integrity leads the way to unity. A design expresses unity through a consistency of grammar, where every component is an integrated part of the harmonious whole, and all is in balance. Grammar is the shape-relationship between the parts. In a unified design we may recognize a motif, certain geometric patterns and

rhythms that carry out the overall theme of the concept. Consistency never precludes variety, but it does mean that everything has a sense of order.

Ideally, unity in architecture carries through every detail, from the structure to the furniture, from planning the site to setting the table for dinner. Each material, each element of a design maintains its own individuality, yet all are fused together to form a unified whole.

Contrast, a quality found in nature, brings interest

Myers residence—the ground itself is a basic component of the building.

Above: *Myers residence—
Organic architecture is
an integral part of the
landscape.*

Right: *Myers residence—
the part is to the whole as
the whole is to the part.*

to unity. In architecture, there are the dualities of open versus intimate space, symmetry versus asymmetry. There are many other contrasts: simple and complex, formal and informal, tall and low, broad and narrow, light and dark, smooth and textured.

Architecture involves many disciplines: civil and structural engineering, mechanical, electrical, lighting, acoustical, interiors, landscaping, and many other sciences. Because of this complexity, there is the danger of a design becoming fragmented. To overcome this, an architect needs to have some fundamental knowledge of every discipline so as to integrate them into a design concept.

Although the conductor of a symphony orchestra may be unable to play every musical instrument, he must know the nature of each and appreciate its potential. So it is with the architect, who needs to understand the role of every participant in the design and construction process. Teamwork needs to be integrative. When every member works in synchronization, the result is unity.

When integrity and unity underlie every aspect, another dimension is invoked. The building gains a spiritual quality. It is impossible to define what it is in some buildings that gives them an almost mystical aura, but the magic grows from honesty, beauty, and harmony. These qualities appeal to both our physical senses and our spirituality.

Sims Residence—architecture that enriches human values.

40

HUMANITY AND SPIRIT

The architect is the master of the elements: earth, air, fire, light and water. Space, motion and gravitation are his palette; the sun, his brush; his concern, the heart of humanity.

—FLLW

What are the qualities that humanize architecture? For space to be friendly and inviting as well as useful, it needs to relate to the nature of human beings. Our size is an essential factor. Buildings that are used by people (as opposed to warehouses, barns, and hangars) need to be in human scale. A building may be very large, but a sense of scale can always be achieved and will make a space more relaxed and comfortable. While tall ceilings are appropriate to the proportion of large spaces, we also need intimate spaces. An aspect of scale usually overlooked is the relationship of people to a space when they are seated or lying down—positions in which we spend more time than we do standing up. The scale of children is seldom considered.

In the past, cathedrals were scaled to divinity and government buildings were scaled to display the power of authority. Today, many commercial structures ignore human scale. It is notably missing in residential designs, where larger-than-life scale is often meant to impress the neighbors rather than nurture the family.

Introducing some lower ceilings to contrast with higher ceilings helps to preserve a sense of human scale. Humanity in architecture also comes through the choice of materials. Most building materials are "cold"—steel, concrete, and glass, for instance. Combining them with "warmer" materials, such as wood and fabric, will soften them. Warm colors and textures add to our ways to humanize our buildings.

Some forms and shapes tend to be more sympathetic to the shape of our bodies than others. Curved or faceted shapes tend to be more comfortable than square shapes (because our bodies are curved, not square). A curved chair is usually more comfortable than a square one. Sharp angles in a building may even appear threatening. This does not mean that square or angular shapes are poor choices, only that recognition needs to be given to ways to harmonize them with the sensitivities the human body. Our physical body is a relatively delicate thing compared with the strength and durability of most building materials.

Indoor planting areas, an intimate connection between interior space and outdoor gardens, natural daylight, and fresh air, natural materials—all help humanize architecture.

There are no forms, sizes, colors, or textures that must be excluded, as long as consideration is given to the idea that architecture should be in concord with the both the human body and the human spirit.

On a larger scale, a sense of humanity should apply to a city. The urban environment should be more benevolent than intimidating. Yet humane architecture is more often found in small towns, country villages, and rural homes than in a metropolitan or suburban context. In the country, houses are less crowded and closer to nature. In a large city, with its pressures of crowding and

El Tohono Conference Center—recognizing the value of humanizing the workspace.

fast life, there is an urgent need for both the urban plan and the buildings to express a humane quality.

As we moved through the industrial and atomic ages to the age of information, science and technology became increasingly more sophisticated, changing and extending our lives. In our hands now lie the intelligence and ingenuity of thousands of inventive people. We have more time for recreation and leisure and can communicate much more easily. Labor saving devices give us a freedom that we never had two hundred years ago. The power of machines, and the ingenuity that we have put into them, allows us to create an architecture that could never have existed in times past.

But machines, as we know, have another side. Tireless, infinitely stronger than humans, able to do what we cannot do or do not have the time, energy, or inclination to do, it is easy to view them as more than merely tools in our hands. But machines have no heart, no spirit. Sadly, we often use them in bad ways, to create implements of destruction.

Yet humanity prevails. When the human spirit senses a threat, it responds. Every day, our interest in art, religion, ethics, and our human potential grows stronger.

Humanity in architecture took a steep decline during the years of the International, Modern, and Postmodern Styles, as these fashions went in and out of favor. The enduring public appreciation of organic architecture through and beyond those decades is evidence of its significance and depth. The abiding quality of organic

architecture is found in its warmth, its humanity. An organic building is an entity of the human spirit, just as a tree or flower is an entity of nature.

The spiritual quality of a design cannot be separated from the quality of beauty. Though it may seem intangible, indescribable, it is nevertheless recognizable. It is the profound element that characterizes great architecture.

It has become appallingly clear that our technology has surpassed our humanity.

—Albert Einstein

HARMONY WITH THE ENVIRONMENT

It is in the nature of any organic building to grow from its site, to come out of the ground into the light, the ground itself always held as a basic component part of the building. The land is the simplest form of architecture. Buildings, too, are creatures of the earth and sun.

—FLLW

Harmony with the environment is a broad principle that is linked to all the other principles. All architecture needs to be sensitive to the forces of nature—the climate, wind, sun, and precipitation. They are the main reason that we require shelter. Architecture must also respect some irrepressible forces: hurricanes, earthquakes, fire, floods, landslides, and avalanches. When we try to control this sort of energy it has a way of mocking our efforts.

In the universe, gravity is an inevitable and incessant force. On earth, it exerts its relentless pull on every object, even air. Its force affects the shape of our designs. It tends to flatten everything, and so makes the horizontal line the line of rest and repose. Horizontal lines and planes in architecture acknowledge the force of gravity and relate a building to the plane of the earth. Vertical lines are lines in balance with the force of gravity, but structures must also recognize the horizontal force exerted by wind and earthquakes.

Ingersoll Residence—of the hill and not on the hill

A design should also pay respect to, and be formed by, the particular features of its site—the topography and landforms, rocks, water, and vegetation. When the environment includes other buildings, we need to consider how to harmonize with them. Humanity is also a part of the landscape, as are all creatures. Every time we erect a structure we are taking a hand in creation.

The fundamental function of a structure is to provide shelter from the elements, protection from the changing circumstances of weather—cold and heat, light and darkness, sun and rain. Shelter is an elemental necessity, so important that it virtually directs the major components of a design, shaping the roof and walls. Expressing a sense of shelter in a design is an honest response to this reality. The sense of shelter in a design comes from its depth dimension, especially through roof overhangs, which create shade. Overhangs keep the sun and rain off walls and glass

Above: *Spring Green Restaurant—its form grows from its site, in sympathy with its surroundings.*

Right: *Shepherd residence —integral to site, environment, and the life of its inhabitants.*

surfaces, increasing comfort and saving energy. Ever-changing shadow and shade patterns add appeal and variety to architecture.

A building should be a natural circumstance on the land, harmonious with and even enhancing its environment, making the landscape more beautiful. A structure should relate to its terrain, be it flat, sloping, or challenging. It is usually better not to build directly on top of a landform. When we build on top of a hill, we lose the hill. By building on its side, we save the best part of the hill to enjoy. A building that nestles into its site becomes a natural part of the land.

Our initial perception of the environment comes from views. By establishing the optimum location and orientation of a building, scenic views are embraced while unwanted views and noises are buffered. In the city it is often impossible, or at least difficult, to obtain a scenic view. If the vista only includes other buildings, the solution may be to internalize views. The inner courtyard and the atrium are ways to accomplish this. Buildings should consider their relationship to each other, and every building should be a good neighbor.

Whenever we crowd our buildings too closely together, we create a dissonance with the environment, not only visually but also through air and noise pollution. The reason for crowding is inevitably an economical one—the high cost of land and infrastructure. Yet what we pay in terms of the impact on our health and happiness seems a much higher price in the long run. The answer is lower density through decentralization, providing more sense of space and freedom. Human beings are also a part of the environment, and human scale is an essential determinant in architecture.

Form should be a consequence of space and its intended use. When the form of a building is inspired

Vail Pass Highway—a reverence for the natural environment.

by the forms of nature that surround it, it will be a natural event in the landscape. Landforms, slopes, and the shapes of nature will ask for, and suggest, sympathetic building forms.

Another link between a building and its site lies in the choice of materials and the way we use them. Materials relate to the environment through color and texture. Apart from water, there are few things in nature with reflective surfaces. Because glass has a very high degree of reflectance in the sun, it needs to be used with care. Buildings that send out a blinding glare from reflected sunlight and add heat to nearby buildings are a serious problem. The easiest way to mitigate reflectance is to shade the glass. Other reflective materials, such as polished metals, present similar problems.

Architecture should be designed to make people look well and feel good, and light, a primary force of the universe, is the beautifier of architecture. The sun brings us both light and heat, and it can generate electricity through photovoltaics. But sunlight is both beneficial and detrimental. Glare and heat need to be controlled. To achieve the best advantage of daylight, a building must be properly orientated. Unfortunately, the standard city grid pattern provides no advantage in this regard. The course of the sun at any time of the day and geographic location is predictable, and the design of a building should utilize and control daylight and minimize the need for artificial light.

In organic architecture, we seek to create a balance of light. It is easier on the eyes and makes everything look better. By bouncing light—from the ground, the underside of roof overhangs, light shelves, or decks, and the ceiling, we can diffuse the light and reduce glare. The best way to light a building at night is to emulate daylight in as natural a way as possible. This means keeping the color of light close to daylight and diffusing it by indirect lighting. Ambient light is then supplemented with task lighting. Sophisticated control systems are now more affordable and pay for themselves by saving energy.

After years of ignorance about how civilization is destroying our natural environment, in the past decade we have begun to awaken to our responsibility to planet Earth. Architecture that is organic is energy conservative and sustainable, a "green" architecture, responsible for energy conservation, recycling of materials, and non-toxic building materials. It is more concerned with quality than quantity. Responsive to new materials and methods, it uses technology as a tool in the service of people—the means but not the end.

As we eventually deplete fossil fuels, we will have to depend entirely on renewable energy sources such as the sun, wind, hydroelectric, geothermal, and nuclear.

Being out of harmony with the environment affects our health. We have long overlooked the effects of chemical and electromagnetic pollution. Emissions from many building materials, together with poorly designed air conditioning systems, are detrimental to our well being. The use of plastics, laminates, and glues, combined with sealed buildings and recycled air, exposes our lungs to unhealthy chemicals. The electromagnetic effect of TV, cellular phones, and other electronic equipment is another cause for concern.

Through our neglect of the environment we have done great harm to our planet. Forest and field have been assaulted, the earth scarred, the ozone layer pierced. Both the earth and the human body have tremendous recuperative powers, but both can be destroyed by abuse. While industry begins to address these concerns, there are some simple, common sense things that we can do now, such as better filters in our mechanical systems and more fresh air from windows. The term "green architecture" means harmony with the environment.

The earth does not belong to us—we belong to the earth.
—Chief Seattle

There are no passengers on Spaceship Earth, everybody's crew.
—Marshall McLuhan

SPACE, FORM, AND
THE THIRD DIMENSION

The reality of the building does not consist of roof and walls but in the space within to be lived in.

—Lao-tse

This quotation is a paraphrase of the Chinese philosopher, Lao-tse, who was born about 600 BC, and wrote with poetic insight. Yet architects of the Western world did not consider this concept of inner space. Architecture, as it was practiced up until the start of the twentieth century, was mostly a matter of copying and adapting the formulas and prescribed appearances of classical styles. The concept of space was missing because, to a large extent, buildings were designed from the outside. The exterior was not a consequence of inner space but a façade within which rooms were arranged. The size of rooms was limited because floor and roof spans were severely limited by the available structural materials—stone, brick, and wood. Windows were holes punched in walls.

The advent of wrought iron, steel, and reinforced concrete made an enormous difference in the ability to create large, open spaces. The invention of plate glass brought light into buildings and allowed a visu-

Lykes Residence—space is the continual becoming, the invisible fountain of rhythms.

47

Desert Arc—a seamless flow of space from indoors to outdoors.

Desert Arc—the concept of open space is the liberation of architecture.

al connection between indoor and outdoor space. Yet despite these great new possibilities, architecture still tended towards box-like forms, rooms being just boxes within a bigger box.

Wright pioneered the use of these new materials and structural methods. As he did away with the box, both in plan and elevation, a new sense of space emerged, walls became screens, and a sense of freedom entered architecture. Space no longer needed to be static and contained, but could flow freely. This idea of plasticity was new to architecture, though not to nature.

Space serves the needs of different activities, and buildings, except for some special-use types like warehouses, must respond to the dynamics of human movement and activity. A building is often very complex in terms of movement of people and goods, and an understanding of flow and function is basic. When Wright gave his view that Louis Sullivan's dictum, "Form follows function" should really be "Form and function are one," he was expressing the need for integration. Design from within outward, said Wright, who once remarked that one of the first organic architects was Christ, because he told us that "the kingdom of God is within you."

In an organic design, the plan is an effective organization of space that accommodates the various functions of the building. The form of the building is a three-dimensional consequence of the plan. A

49

Paradise Peak West— a new sense of space emerges.

building conceived as a three-dimensional entity will have design integrity.

There is a natural hierarchy of space in architecture. In a house, for instance, the living area is naturally the dominant space, its form and mass clearly expressed on the exterior. Other spaces though subordinate will interconnect and relate to each other. The integral flow of space and form are the essence of architecture.

Central to the philosophy of organic architecture is the idea that there should be a sense of discovery of space. This discovery starts at the entrance to a building. Rather than scaling the front door of a building to a heroic level to impress the person who enters, the entrances we design are usually underplayed. This is where the element of human scale is first established. The entrance should not lose anything in quality, but just as a good novel does not reveal its plot on the first

page, the space experience becomes a series of discoveries as one moves into the interior. Architecture is much more interesting if the arrangement of spaces is not too obvious, if there is a surprise and mystery around every corner. The unexpected space experience can add charm and appeal, so a space should seldom be seen in its entirety. Roofs and ceilings can have many levels; high soaring space can be contrasted with low, snug alcoves. Bright, sunny spaces contrast with dark retreats, one interior space can borrow visually from other contiguous spaces through broad openings. Interior and exterior space can be separated by glass but linked visually so that interior space flows outward. Walls can reach out and embrace the landscape. Spatial continuity—the continuous flow of space—gives architecture a magical sense of freedom.

The elements that establish architectural space—the

walls, roofs, and all the details—are given definition by their boundaries, that is, by their edges and corners. In other words, by their terminals. Louis Sullivan passed along a wise observation: "Take care of the terminals and the rest will take care of itself." This applies not just to design but to many things in life. We only look well dressed if our shoes are shined, our fingernails are clean, and our hair is neat. A good opening and a good closing are keys to a successful talk or a story. So the design of corners, edges, and finials becomes important in the creation of space.

Dimensions of an object have height, width, and depth, but what do we mean by depth as an element of interior space? Depth in this case is not thickness but a dimension of space. It leads to the dynamics of space, what we might call spatial interweave, the interpenetration of one space into other spaces, the intersecting and overlapping of spaces. The lack of depth results in static, two-dimensional architecture.

"Façade" buildings are, unfortunately, all too common. We often see them in tract housing, where the street elevation is "fancied up" with some brick or stone, but the sides and back are a sham, made of the cheapest possible materials. A shop that has only a "storefront" seems like a set for a western movie. The modern "glass box" office building is often just a mirrored shell that lacks depth.

In organic architecture, space and form are three-dimensional. Walls become screens that define and differentiate space without confining or destroying it. The depth dimension is the quality that enables architecture to have that intangible but essential quality of spirituality. There is a mystery to nature and life that we seek to understand but can never adequately describe. An organic building, in its third dimension, also has this magic, constantly bringing surprises of beauty. As the sun creates ever-changing patterns of light and shadow, different views of architectural forms and details reveal themselves. Light and shade give life to architecture.

Most things in life we can learn, but it seems that a sense of artistic proportion is something with which we must be born. We can, however, augment whatever

Rocky Mountain National Park Headquarters—its structure is architectural affirmation.

senses we have. A sense of proportion is essential to design, just as it is to life. In life, a sense of proportion will moderate our behavior, help us avoid excess. It will tell us when we have had enough to eat, the right amount of exercise and sleep that we need, and when we should stop talking. It applies to just about everything.

In architecture, it will instinctively work to give proper balance to the sizes and shapes of spaces and forms. Harmony is only achieved when everything is in balance. A sense of proportion will help us avoid either underdoing or overdoing a thing. The great artist is the one who knows just when to stop.

The fairest thing we can experience is the mysterious. It is the fundamental emotion which stands at the cradle of true art and true science.

—Albert Einstein

Golden Rondelle—steel brings continuity, new forms, and freedom to architecture.

STRUCTURAL CONTINUITY

Organic architecture is the scientific art of making structure express ideas, the art of building wherein aesthetics and construction not only approve but prove each other.
—FLLW

Almost nothing in nature, from the atom to the blade of grass or the giant sequoia, is fabricated by piling one element on top of another. Yet this is the way that most of mankind constructed buildings. In nature, we see that the components of an entity are knit together. This is continuity, or plasticity, where structure is integrated, inseparable from form. For example, in the chambered nautilus seashell it is apparent that structure and form are inseparable. The structure of the shell is a direct consequence of its shape, and the arrangement of its inner chambers. These chambers function as floats or ballast tanks, and their shape gives strength to an extremely frag-

ile shell. There is both spatial continuity and structural continuity. Form, function, and structure are one.

In the human body, our skeleton is the structural system, marvelously adapted to serve our needs for articulated motion. Our hands and fingers provide a strong grip or perform incredibly complex and delicate movements. Unless we allow our bodies to get drastically out of shape, we can recognize how our form and movement are directly and intelligently related to our structural system.

An organic structural concept has this same sense of continuity. It is an integral part of the space-form idea, with structure taken into account as an integral part of the design concept. Organic architecture is the synthesis of structure and form, with form united to its function.

The traditional post and beam method of construction, a horizontal beam resting on a vertical column, lacks continuity. It also lends itself to the sim-

plest form of enclosure, which is a box, walls with holes cut in for windows. A box may be ornamented, it may be surrounded by columns and have all sorts of features applied to it, but it is still a box, and confinement doesn't express the spirit of freedom that is the essence of our democracy.

Frank Lloyd Wright was the first architect to "destroy the box" in architecture: "As a young architect I began to feel imposed upon by this sense of enclosure which you went into and there you were—

boxed, crated. I began to see what was the matter: structurally, the box puts the supports at the far corners. I was engineer enough to know that the place where the building can be most economically supported is *in* from the corners."

This revolutionary way of thinking brought forth the cantilever. Made possible by the use of steel, it renders the corner support unnecessary. As the corners open up, the box disappears. Floors and roofs, no longer confined, extend out into space. Roofs can

San Jose Community Theater—great distances spanned economically.

Spiral stair at the law offices of Lewis and Roca —plasticity of form is natural to reinforced concrete.

become broad and protective brows that provide shelter and shade.

Two dramatic pioneering examples demonstrate the effectiveness of structural continuity, of integrating form and structure. In 1914, when Wright designed the Imperial Hotel in Tokyo, he took a clue from nature—when the wind blows, the grass leaf bends and then springs back up. Instead of designing a rigid structure to resist earthquake forces, he made the foun-

dations and structural connections flexible. The floors were balanced cantilevers. In 1923, the Great Kanto earthquake leveled the city, killing an estimated 74,000 persons and destroying some 700,000 homes. The Imperial Hotel stood undamaged.

In 1936, when he designed the dendriform columns for the Johnson Wax Administration Building, he could not get a construction permit because the building codes said the column could not carry its design load of twelve tons. A dramatic test of an actual column demonstrated it could carry sixty tons before it failed. After that, engineers revised their formulas.

Today we have a multitude of structural techniques available to us. Reinforced concrete can be precast, prestressed, or post-tensioned. Steel comes in many strengths and shapes. Lumber can be laminated and reconstituted. We have carbon fiber and plastics. Computers come to our aid by performing incredibly complicated structural calculations. There is almost no form that we can imagine which we cannot build. The consolidation of skeleton and form in architecture creates a sense of unity, and in this unity lies its integrity. Walls, floors, and ceilings can flow into one another, become component parts of each other, all part of a stream of continuity. Nature, with its millions of years of patient creation and invention, still teaches us about continuity and the miraculous integration of shape and structure.

An organic form grows its structure out of conditions as a plant grows out of the soil. Both unfold similarly within.

—FLLW

THE NATURE OF MATERIALS

The materials of which the building is built will go far to determine its appropriate mass, its outline and, especially, proportion.

—FLLW

A common misunderstanding of this principle is that it means that the materials that you should use in a building are ones that can be found naturally on the site. When appropriate materials can be found on the site, so much the better, but that is not what is meant by the nature of materials. The word "nature" in this context refers to the individual attributes, or special qualities, that characterize each material and give it distinction. Materials are the resources of architec-

ture. Every material has its own significance, its own potential, and its own limitations. It has its own unique appearance, rough and finished, and one material should not be made to imitate another. We should respect the essential qualities of each material, find its true nobility, and use it honestly in ways that are appropriate to its nature.

There are many characteristics to consider: strength,

Stone wall at Taliesin—to know how to lay stone, study it in its natural state.

Right: *Office for Thorpe Interiors. Strong in compression, bricks are a natural material for arches.*

Below: *Harbortown Inn—tile roofs offer durability.*

durability, plasticity, workability, weight, hardness, resistance to water, texture, color, transparency, and economics. The best way to get a feel for the nature of a material is to work it with your hands.

Masonry and Tile. Brick, concrete block, and stone are solid, durable, and strong when resisting compression. They will sustain heavy vertical loads. Masonry units may be formed into arches or domes, which transfer loads to the side, but unless reinforcing is added they lack the ability to resist tensile forces. The character of their inherent massiveness should be expressed in a design.

Brick is the earliest of man-made materials. It comes from a natural earth substance, clay, which is shaped and baked by fire (adobe bricks are sun-baked). The dimensions of this shape become a small repeated unit mathematically related to the larger unit geometry of the structure. When we use brick, we color the mortar to match the brick, striking the vertical joints flush and raking out the horizontal joints. This makes the wall

First Christian Church—the economy of pouring repetitive units from the same mold.

appear more monolithic and, at the same time, emphasizes the horizontal line, the line of repose.

Stone is one of nature's wonderful materials and comes in many types. Some, like marble and granite, can be polished. To know how to lay stone in a wall, study it in its natural state. In a stone quarry we see the characteristics of each type of stone. Sedimentary rocks like sandstone or limestone are stratified into ledges. When placed in a wall, they will appear most natural if they are laid in a stratum-like manner.

Tiles are made of clay, stone, or manufactured materials and come in all sorts of shapes, colors, and textures. Since they are relatively small units in size, they can cover curved surfaces.

Concrete, capable of being formed into almost any shape we can imagine, changed the face of architecture. Used by the Romans, it had only limited use until steel was added. When concrete, which has a high compressive strength, is combined with steel, which is high in tensile strength, we have reinforced concrete, a material that resists both types of forces and has true plasticity. There are many ways to manufacture and improve concrete, such as air-entrainment, dewatering, gunite, prestressing, and post tensioning. It is interesting to note that the first patent for this reinforced concrete was issued to Joseph Monier in 1867, the year that Frank Lloyd Wright was born.

Steel can be shaped in several ways—cast, rolled, flattened into sheets, or drawn into slender wires. Most effective and economical when used in tension, its amazing tensile strength is demonstrated in a suspension or stayed-cable bridge. Its properties are uniform and its strength a mathematical certainty, so there is no need of waste. It has tenuity, a characteristic seen in nature in the lightness, strength, and continuity of a spider web. Its drawback is that it rusts when exposed to weather (unless it is Corten steel).

Plaster is a fluid material while it is being applied. Easily adapted to almost any shape, it is susceptible to a variety of textures. When color is mixed into the plaster or stucco, it looks better than a coat of paint. Although plaster is subject to cracks, synthetic materials with plasticity can be added to help overcome this inherent weakness. Gypsum board has virtually replaced plaster (except where there are compound curves), and is easier, cheaper, and faster to install.

Model of Belmont Park Pavilion—the technology of a steel suspension bridge applied to architecture.

Above: *Dodge Residence —mitered glass corners open up space, do away with confinement.*

Right: *Pearl Palace— plastic offers possibilities for both curved shapes and light transfer.*

Glass is a remarkable material because to some extent it is invisible. It allows for views both in and out, introducing a sense of freedom to architecture. The daylight that it brings is a great blessing but something to control, since along with the beneficence of light and warmth comes unwanted glare and heat. Clear glass also creates a lack of privacy. Reflections from the exterior surface of glass are a problem because they reflect both heat and glare to other buildings and to people. Office buildings with all-glass façades are a prime example. Shading the glass is a natural way to mitigate some of these problems. Glass may be tinted or layered, and now we have "intelligent" glass that keeps heat and ultraviolet rays out but allows daylight to enter. Future development will bring down the cost of a new type of glass that can be "tuned" to different colors, opacities, and reflectance.

Plastic is, of course, a synthetic material, and one that is being used more and more in a variety of ways as a building material. Being fluid in its manufacturing process, it can be given almost any shape, color, texture, or degree of transparency. Plastic is certainly the material of the future. Science will produce new types of plastic with a wider range of uses.

Wood. A carpenter knows the essence of wood: its strength, the different shrinkage factors between "with the grain" and "cross grain," and the beauty of different slices and veneers. The beauty of wood lies in its variety of grains and color tones. They express the fact that it was once alive. Like all living materials, it is subject to decay and must be maintained. By laminating wood we have created plywood and glulam beams. By combining wood chips with plastic we have produced particle board.

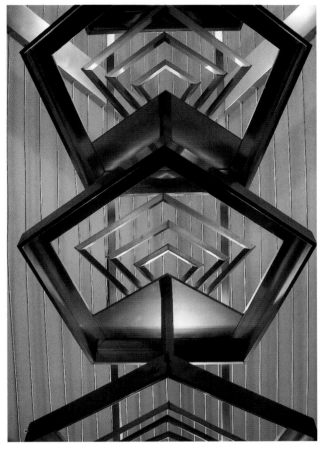

Far left: *The cross of the Ascension Lutheran Church is made of gold-anodized aluminum pentagonal shapes attached to tension wires.*

Left: *Hillside Studio— wood trusses, designed as an effective and beautiful way to span space.*

These are just some of the materials that we use. There are many others—copper, stainless steel, fiberglas, fabrics, and hundreds more.

Recognizing the individuality and distinction of each material, we seldom allow the surface of one material to be set flush with the surface of another material. If a brick wall meets a wood wall in the same plane, there will be an offset where the two materials join, even if it is only an inch or two. When we use glass, we often cut a slot, or rabbet, in a wall and run clear glass into it. This creates a seamless indoor/outdoor connection.

Our imagination will let us see, in each material, its own inherent characteristics. All materials can be beautiful. Their beauty depends on how well their individual nature is appreciated, and the sensitivity with which they are used in a building. Materials used with integrity and sensitivity produce a beneficence that is hard to come by in other ways—a sense of human warmth. Many people who live or work in an organic building have noted this.

Color is closely related to texture, and color without texture usually has no quality. Whenever we deal with texture, we must consider light. Without light, texture cannot appeal to our sight, only to our touch. In the sunlight, texture takes on a continual change in appearance as the sun strikes it from different angles. In many of the communities which we have master planned, we establish guidelines for colors. These restrict buildings to a palette of appropriate earth tones, and they play a major role harmonizing a community with its environment. If we truly understand the inner nature of a building material, we will use it in an appropriate and honest way to bring out its best features.

ASU Music Building—an educational building that is an inspiration to learning.

CHARACTER

First we shape our buildings; then our buildings shape us.
—Winston Churchill

The character of a design is its essential nature, the distinctive quality that expresses its purpose and meaning. A building's character should be appropriate to its use. The form and shape of a structure should clearly indicate the nature of the activity it serves, be it an office, a bank, a school, or a residence. In simple terms, a school should not look like an office building, nor should an office building look like a factory.

In an abstract way, a building serves as an icon for its purpose, for the activity within. For civic buildings that serve public needs, the building is a symbol of public service; in a democratic society we would expect it to reflect the spirit of democracy. The character of a hospital will have some aspect of medical technology, but also evoke a sense of humanity, caring and healing, while the character of a church is, of course, inspirational.

The individual design distinction of a structure also reflects its relationship to its geographic location and its cultural context. A building in a cold, northern climate calls for some difference in character from a building in the south, because both climate and culture influence character.

Many contemporary buildings are unclear about their character. The "International Style" which dominated commercial architecture from 1930 to 1970 was supposed to fit anywhere. This "grand idea" completely ignored variations in culture, geography, terrain, and harmony with the environment. As a result,

Far left: *Lincoln Tower—a place of business should be both efficient and humane.*

Left: *St. Mary's Catholic Church—inspiring hope, compassion, and love.*

it really didn't fit anywhere. Nor does the so-called "Postmodern Style," which has produced many buildings that lack character. Buildings in New York, Hong Kong, or London often look the same, with no regard for their function or unique cultural and environmental conditions. The significance of their appearance is confusing—is it a hospital, a school, or an office building? Character is absent when a bank looks like a house or a Greek temple.

An interesting challenge comes when we design a building in another country, and need to consider its context with the culture of that region. Most cultures have historically developed their own architectural forms, but because of colonialism and the geographical interchange of technology, an architectural mishmash has been created. Each culture of the world has its own distinctive qualities, and some regard for this should be inherent in a modern design. A building in a Native American community, for instance, should respect the cultural heritage of the tribe.

Organic architecture is not about historical styles. Yet a good design will have the quality of style about it, meaning it will have its own intrinsic yet distinct character, a sense of simple elegance. This elegance is best when stated quietly, rather than being flaunted.

Just as character defines the individuality of a human being, gives us depth and interest, so it defines the distinctiveness of a building. We talk of strength of character in a person as an essential quality. It denotes integrity, honesty, ethics, resolution, and strength. These qualities are all true for architecture.

We can see character in nature, in every species of animal and plant, in the rocks and mountains, seas and rivers. It extends from the atom to the universe. Character in a building will give it endurance and let it work its beneficial influence on our lives.

BEAUTY AND ROMANCE

Civilization is a way of life; culture is a way of making life beautiful.

—FLLW

The significance of beauty in architecture cannot be overstated. "Beauty is truth, truth beauty," wrote Keats, and in beauty is the highest kind of morality. Beauty is essential to architecture because architecture influences us every moment of our lives. Aesthetics and ethics are both words that come from the Greek language, and the Greeks did not distinguish the sphere of aesthetics from the sphere of ethics. The aesthetic element of a design is its connection to divinity. Nature is filled with beauty, and our environment is a priceless heritage. When what we build complements nature, we have fulfilled a higher responsibility

When we talk about human virtues, about great acts that a person does, we say they are beautiful. Beauty is really the expression of inner experience. We all know people who may not be physically very attractive but who have an inner glow that transcends their appearance. This is something that they have created within themselves. Just as real beauty in a human being is a quality that comes from inside, so it is with architecture. It cannot be applied from the outside.

In the hands of the architect is placed a great opportunity, the possibility to perform something miraculous. Out of inanimate materials we can grow a thing of beauty.

One Sunday morning, Wright talked to his apprentices about learning to distinguish between the curious and the beautiful. "A flower is beautiful, we say, but why? Because in its geometry and its sensuous qualities, it is an embodiment and significant

Pearl Palace at night— organic architecture is essentially romantic.

Annunciation Greek Orthodox Church— beauty is the highest kind of morality.

expression of that precious something in ourselves which we instinctively know to be life. An eye looking out upon us from the great inner sea of beauty— a proof of the eternal harmony in the nature of the universe which is too vast and intimate and real for the mere intellect to seize.

"When we perceive a thing to be beautiful, it is because we instinctively recognize the rightness of the thing. This means that we have revealed to us a glimpse of something essential of the fiber of our own nature. Artists make this revelation to us through a deeper insight. Their power to visualize conceptions being greater than our own, a flash of truth stimulates us, and we have a vision of harmonies not understood today, though perhaps it will be tomorrow.

"Human beings can be beautiful. If they are not

San Marcos in the Desert —its poetry is architectural romance.

beautiful it is entirely their own fault. It is what they do to themselves that makes them ugly. The longer I live the more beautiful life becomes. If you foolishly ignore beauty you will soon find yourself without it. Your life will be impoverished. But if you invest in beauty, it will remain with you all the days of your life."

The magic of beauty is something we can appreciate, something that stirs our feelings, but is not easy to explain. Words, in fact, may detract from the enjoyment of its mystery. When people share the delight of a beautiful moment—a flower, a sunset, a song, or a child, they communicate their joy with something other than words. Although beauty is to some extent subjective (in the eye of the beholder), we may agree that beauty is a universal quality of nature. The quest of organic architecture is to search for an objective beauty, a search for truth. One of the things we teach young architects at Taliesin is the importance of sensitivity to details in daily life, such as placing fresh flowers on the dining tables. We urge them to be constantly conscious of the beauty of their surroundings, to seek opportunities to create something beautiful.

What do we mean by romance in architecture? The meaning of many words seems to change with time. Advertising has contributed to this circumstance. There is hardly an adjective in our lexicon that has not been used to describe the benefit of some product like soap or toothpaste. How can a word like "romance" retain its meaning when it is used with such sentimentality to describe a new perfume? Words, like people, are the victims of pollution.

Why is romance so natural to an organic architecture? Romance is an attribute of human emotions, a poetic and spiritual quality, a compelling force of joy. In anything beautiful there is always an element of mystery, an aspect that defies finite analysis. It is a virtue perceptible in nature, in the magic of a flower, a sunset or a mountain. It is a quality of love. When architecture is based on ideas, imagination, and nature, romance is inherent in the design. Imagination is an adventure and romance its natural consequence.

Devotion to beauty and the creation of beautiful things is the test of all great civilizations.

—Oscar Wilde

Theilen Residence—
the level plane is the
line of repose.

SIMPLICITY AND REPOSE

To know what to leave out and what to put in; just where and how, that is to have been educated in the knowledge of simplicity.

—FLLW

Simplicity in architecture is the clear and straightforward expression of a building's essential nature. One of the tenets of modern architecture, formulated by Mies Van der Rohe, is "Less is more." This notion was born at a time when buildings were covered by decorations, carvings, and moldings, ad infinitum. Architecture was in desperate need of simplification; it was time for a clean-up. But like many reactions, the pendulum swung too far. The result was minimalism, with buildings becoming sterile, flat, and uninteresting.

The qualities of simplicity and serenity are evident everywhere in nature. Wright made a clear distinction between elimination and simplicity: "Five lines where three are enough is always stupidity. Nine pounds where three are sufficient is obesity. But to eliminate expressive words in speaking or writing, words that intensify or vivify meaning, is not simplicity. Nor is elimination in architecture simplicity. It may be, and usually is, stupidity."

Nothing better exemplifies true simplicity than the ancient woodblock print of Japan. In Japanese prints we find that the supreme principle of aesthetics is elimination of the insignificant, discovery of the essence. This process is true simplification, achieving a clean work of art where nothing can be added, nothing subtracted, without detriment to the whole.

Wright discussed simplicity in his autobiography: "Organic simplicity might everywhere be seen producing significant character in nature. I was more than familiar with it on the farm. All around me I might see beauty in growing things and, by a little painstaking effort, learn how they grew to be beautiful. None was ever insignificant. Only as a feature or any part becomes a harmonious element in the harmonious whole does it arrive at the state of simplicity.

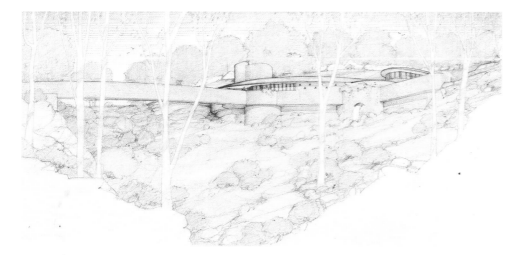

Beck Residence—simplicity means the clean and direct expression of an idea.

Waikapu Clubhouse—grace and concord arise from simplicity and repose.

"But simplicity is not in itself an end nor is it a matter of the side of a barn but rather an entity with a graceful beauty in its integrity from which discord, and all that is meaningless, has been eliminated. A wild flower is truly simple. An excessive love of detail has ruined more fine things from the standpoint of fine art or fine living than any one human shortcoming—it is hopelessly vulgar. Too many houses, when they are not little stage settings or scene paintings, are mere notion stores, bazaars, or junk-shops. Decoration is dangerous unless you understand it thoroughly and are satisfied that it means something good in the scheme as a whole;

for the present, you are usually better off without it. Merely that it 'looks rich' is no justification for the use of ornament. Simplicity is a consequence, never a cause.

"Repose is a quality of architecture essential to harmony with nature and humanity. When man wants to rest, he puts his body in a position where he no longer has to exert effort to resist gravitational force. He is then in a state of repose, a natural condition if he is not in motion. The landscape has this sense of tranquillity. Simplicity and repose give architecture grace and concord.

"Build buildings that you feel when you come into them, that have repose. You want a sense of human dignity and worth in what you feel as you live in them, and what they do to you because buildings must be experienced. You can't listen to them as you would music and you can't look at them the way you do a painting. Simplicity and repose are qualities that measure the true value of any work of art."

The concept of repose in a building is essential as it responds to the ever-present force of gravity, but it does not deny the need for dynamic space. In an organic building, dynamic forms and space still recognize the force of gravity. The Guggenheim Museum in New York City is an example of a dynamic, exciting space that still has repose. The spiral ramp that expands outward as it rises is a powerful statement of motion. The simplicity of the design, the mono-material, vertical fins, and the harmony of its curved shapes create a sense of stability and rest.

The horizontal line is the line of tranquillity. It is the line that gravity gives to water, the line of the prairie, the line that we humans take at rest. A building relates to the flat plane of the land through an expression of horizontality. Roofs that have generous overhanging eaves with flat soffit planes will relate the structure to the earth, providing a sense of shelter and repose.

We no longer live in simple terms, in simple times or places. Life is a more complex struggle now. It is now valiant to be simple; a courageous thing even to want to be simple. It is a spiritual thing to comprehend what simplicity means.

—FLLW

DECENTRALIZATION

Little by little people are going to become more and more dissatisfied with increasing urban pressures.

—FLLW

Decentralization could improve the quality of life in our big cities, in our government, and in our educational system. We need cities that are less dense and more human. We need less central government and

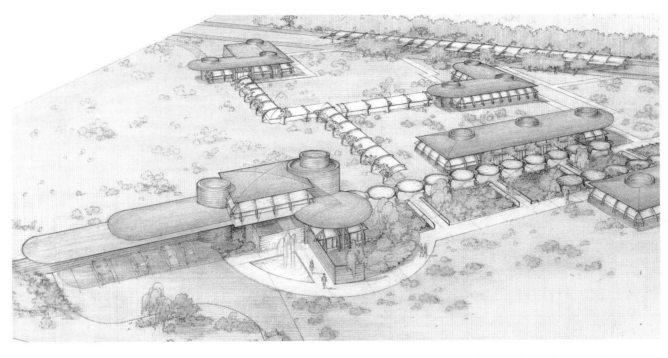

Blood Services Offices—decentralization resolves congestion.

more at state, county and local levels, where the needs of the people can be served more closely. We need smaller colleges and universities, where teacher and student can connect.

In the last half of the twentieth century, many aspects of how we live, work and enjoy leisure changed radically. The advance of science and technology brought mixed blessings. The automobile and jet airplane give us the benefits of rapid travel but also create health problems—air pollution from cars and contagion in airplanes. Newspapers, radio, TV, telecommunications, and computers bring us a

wealth of information, but now we find ourselves informed beyond our capacity. The anxiety of trying to keep up with the rapid pace of life allows little time for reflection.

Apart from some new Asian mega-cities, virtually all of the big cities in the world were established hundreds or even thousands of years ago. Laid out before the advent of the automobile, they expanded haphazardly, driven by economic pressures. Although governments work hard to control growth patterns, establish zoning, and provide utilities and services, many large cities are gradually strangling themselves. A multitude of problems confronts us: little sunshine, air and noise pollution, traffic jams, a lack of parking, and deterioration of the infrastructure. High rent, homeless people, overcrowding, and ugliness confront us and guarantee crime. The frenetic pace of life brings stress and sickness.

The world population continues to expand at an ever-increasing rate. Health care, drugs, and surgery increase fertility at one end of life and extend our life span at the other. There are more people alive on the

*Spanish Reef Club—
every individual needs
space, quiet, and clean air.*

planet today than have existed on earth over the past five thousand years, and all of us are consumers. People are at last waking up to the realization that for years we have been depleting our natural resources and destroying much of our natural environment.

Concerns over life in the city have been stewing for years and have proliferated to a point approaching critical mass. If we do not change our cities through the conscious will of the people, they will be spontaneously changed by default.

For city dwellers, relief comes if they can briefly escape the confining walls of their self-imposed incarceration. A day in the country with fresh air, sunshine, peace and quiet gives us restoration. The need for herding together has long since passed. In medieval times, people were forced to live compactly for reasons of safety; towns were fortresses. Without quick transportation and good communication systems they needed to be within walking distance of a market. It was often less expensive to live in the city. Conditions are quite different now.

An answer to the problem lies in decentralization. Most large cities are struggling to keep their downtown area alive and are forced to decentralize because high rent and a lack of parking are discouraging. Neighborhood shopping centers and the business parks are indicators of the need for smaller-scale units. The home office, now possible for many because of computers and the Internet is an example of effective decentralization.

Along with the idea of democracy and freedom for every individual goes the need for space. Why not create cities that are smaller, quieter, with more green open space? As we prepare to take up the challenge of a new century we have at our side some remarkable tools and learning experiences that were unavailable to city planners fifty years ago.

The metropolis will always have an essential role in civilization, but it will take a huge effort to renovate infrastructures, resolve pollution, parking, and transportation problems, and humanize the urban environment.

FREEDOM

Listen to the still small voice of conscience. A man's conscience is really the mainspring of his soul. Freedom without it is dangerous.

—FLLW

What is more precious to a good life on earth than freedom? For centuries humankind has fought and died for it. Yet freedom was a stranger to architecture until the invention of glass, steel, reinforced concrete, and other modern materials.

Of all the governmental systems established in this world, only democracy, with its commitment to equal opportunity for each individual, freedom of expression, and belief in the essential dignity and worth of the individual, has endured and flourished.

While we may appreciate the spirit of self-determination inherent in democracy and cherish our freedom, we must deplore the fact that so much architecture does not express a sense of liberty. The greatest crusader for freedom in architecture was Frank Lloyd Wright, who said, "Organic architecture is architecture of democracy; the freedom of the indi-

House of the Future—a sense of liberty is intrinsic to organic architecture.

73

Monona Terrace—freedom cannot be given, it is something within you.

vidual becomes the motive for society and government. A sense of liberty is intrinsic to an organic architecture." Freedom cannot be given and it cannot be taken. It is a spirit within each of us. Freedom itself does not come free, but carries innate obligations. Its partner is responsibility. This is true in life and it is true in architecture.

Even today, when we can readily create free and open space, many buildings are designed as boxes. This is the case in the design of most houses in America. What symbol can one find that is less expressive of our liberation than a box?

Freedom in architecture is achieved through the continuous flow of space. We can have continuity of space rather than containment. Instead of rectangular rooms, with holes cut in walls for doors and windows, we have an open plan, where one space flows into other spaces. Walls become more like screens. Opaque, translucent, or transparent, they define rather than confine space.

Glass allows us to make a seamless connection between indoor and outdoor space. When we eliminate the corner post and use mitered glass in a corner we create a sense of freedom. The open space plan has done more to improve architecture in this century than any other thing. Besides being functionally efficient and aesthetically pleasing, its sense of freedom is a sign of hope to the spirit of mankind. With the world gradually moving closer to global democracy, freedom of space in architecture is a great symbol for world peace and the freedom of all humanity.

Hillside Villas—a sense of free space starts with the open plan.

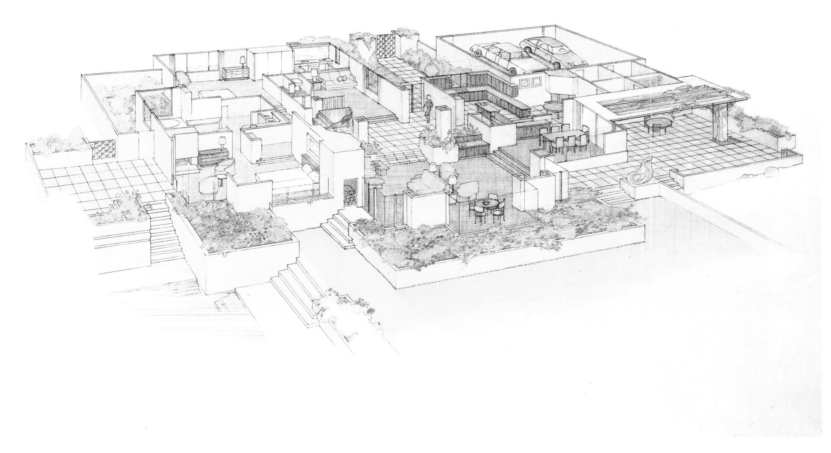

TALIESIN ARCHITECTS

*Taliesin Architects in 1959—continuing
the exploration of organic architecture.*

Frank Lloyd Wright left behind a group of dedicated apprentices and associates who worked with him in his professional practice, some for as long as twenty-seven years. The Taliesin Fellowship was one of the main reasons that Wright was able to be so incredibly productive in his last years, designing over two hundred projects between the ages of eighty-two and ninety-two. After his death on April 11, 1959, most of the senior members of the Fellowship stayed at Taliesin to form the core of the architectural office and the school of architecture.

We incorporated as Taliesin Architects, and our first responsibility was to complete over thirty Wright-designed buildings that were in progress. These included the Guggenheim Museum and the Beth Sholom Synagogue, which were under construction, and others for which we were left design sketches—the Annunciation Greek Orthodox Church, the Corbin Education Center, the Gammage Memorial Auditorium, and the Marin County Civic Center, as well as many houses. We faithfully completed these projects, exercising the same care and attention to

Taliesin Architects studio —forty years of design excellence and innovation.

detail that we did while Wright was alive.

Soon the firm began to receive its own commissions. The size and complexity of the projects grew, and our work expanded across the country and abroad. From the start, we followed the principles set forth by Wright. The nature of organic architecture is one of evolution, and the goals of the firm continue to be the same—to explore ideas, embrace new technology, and seek fresh architectural forms.

Today the staff of over fifty includes fifteen registered architects. The majority of the group are alumni of the Frank Lloyd Wright School of Architecture.

Our headquarters are located at Taliesin West in Scottsdale, Arizona, and we have offices at Taliesin in Spring Green and Madison, Wisconsin. Some of the Taliesin Fellows have independent practices and collaborate with Taliesin Architects on various projects. They run our Associate Offices in California, Colorado, Texas, Tennessee, Florida, and Hawaii.

The services that we provide include architecture, engineering, interior design, landscape architecture, land-use and master planning, as well as integral arts and graphic design. A principal architect, accountable to the client, oversees each project. This principal leads a team that provides the technical excellence and coordination between design and construction. It is the responsibility of each team to ensure that a creative solution is achieved, on time and within the budget. Our goal is to integrate practicality with beauty, so that the owner sees returns in the form of economic construction, low maintenance, and operational efficiency.

One of the aspects of Taliesin Architects that makes us unique and vital is our dedication to education. The studio is a teaching office, serving as a living laboratory for the apprentices of the Frank Lloyd Wright School of Architecture. Apprentices come to us from all

*The studio at Hillside,
Wisconsin—the trusses
create an abstract forest.*

over the world. In the studio, with architects as mentors, the young students gain experience by working on active commissions. The learning process involves every aspect of architecture, engineering, and planning. Apprentices gain hands-on construction experience by working on buildings on the campus of Taliesin and Taliesin West.

The school also serves as a "farm," where we grow our next "crop" of architects. After graduation, some of the young architects join our professional staff, forming the next generation of Taliesin Architects.

As we advance, exploring new ideas and new forms, the atmosphere at Taliesin is filled with a sense of challenge and excitement. As more and more people in the world awaken to the principles of organic architecture and its potential to support human values, we are filled with optimism.

To illustrate the ideas and ideals of organic archi-

tecture here, a representative cross-section has been selected, arranged according to different building types. They illustrate the scope and quality of our work over the past forty years. The variety of these designs demonstrates that the discipline of adherence to principle does not limit the ability of an architect to create fresh and exciting forms.

Although only one architect is noted for each project (usually the principal in charge), there is a closely-knit team that cooperates to shepherd a design from its concept to the completed building. Consideration of space precludes naming the team members. Many of the principals of the firm are listed in the appendix, but there are many people whose names are not mentioned. Design teams include architects, associates, artists, managers, technicians, engineers, and consultants. Although they are not all identified, each member is essential to the success of the project.

There are more than one thousand alumni from Taliesin, most of them practicing architecture in the U.S. and around the world. Their work is a major part of the continuation of organic architecture, but there is insufficient space to include it here. In addition to these Taliesin Fellows, there are many other architects today whose work is based on organic principles.

The constant exploration of fresh ideas and new possibilities is an adventure that keeps our work meaningful and exciting. We have made a commitment to designing humane architecture that is in harmony with its physical environment. Our mission is to embody the fresh spirit of our time and the people we serve. Our focus is the enrichment of life by way of creative design.

There is no true understanding of art without some knowledge of its philosophy.

—FLLW

THE PROJECTS
1959-2000

Gammage Auditorium—its design transforms space and transcends time.

CULTURAL

Van Wezel Performing Arts Center — a chandelier of Tivoli lights illuminates a stairwell.

Many of the architects at Taliesin have some talent in the performing arts, and our interest and broad experience in culture affords us special insight when we design theaters and auditoriums. As part of our community life, we operate three of our own theaters, one at Taliesin and two at Taliesin West. These multi-purpose theaters allow us to perform and experiment in music, poetry, dance, drama, and stagecraft. From time to time we present music, drama, dance, and poetry recitals. We set up the theatrical lighting, make our own costumes and scenery. Said *Cue* magazine, "These productions at Taliesin are a rare and beautiful delight. There exists an affinity between architecture and theater because the same design principles are at work in both." Actress Helen Hayes, who gave a guest performance for us in our theater at Taliesin West, said, "I would give anything to perform on this stage."

The centers for performing arts that Taliesin Architects has designed are noted for excellent acoustics, sightlines, ease of exiting, and the integration of theater technology. Equally important, we have built them all within tight budgets. We design a building from the viewpoint of both audience and

Taliesin West Cabaret Theater—a place of enchantment.

American Players Theater —artists reveal truth through a deeper insight.

performer, integrating architecture with the special demands of theater technology—sightlines, acoustics, and lighting.

One of the challenges in designing a theater is harmonizing its function with the form of the building. The problem is complex. The stagehouse itself is just a gigantic filing cabinet to store scenery. The nature of some functions, such as drama or opera, is to create an illusion for the audience, a magic peep show. The audience is separated from the stage, looking into another world. The hall itself must be a clear span, requiring significant structural framing members overhead. The complicated science and art of acoustics, lighting, staging, sightlines, and exit requirements must be resolved and integrated.

Very often theaters are simply squeezed into rectangular forms that bear no relation to the configuration of the audience. The architectural forms of our theater-auditoriums are not boxes, but express a sense of the functions within.

Great art alone can prevent us from becoming spiritually paralyzed by standardization, from being sterilized by mechanical systems and losing the rich and potent sense of life.

—FLLW

GAMMAGE MEMORIAL AUDITORIUM

Tempe, Arizona
Date Completed: 1964
William Wesley Peters, Architect

In 1958, the president of the Arizona State University, Dr. Grady Gammage, asked Frank Lloyd Wright to design an auditorium. He was working on a concept at the time he died. When Dr. Gammage died later in the same year, it was up to Taliesin Architects to finish the project.

It was not easy to get the state legislature to approve funds. The University kept thinking of more things to include in the program: 3,000 seats, multi-purpose use—music ranging from a soloist or string quartet to a symphony orchestra, opera, musicals, ballet, drama, and lectures.

A 40,000–square foot music school was added, to make the total area of Gammage 135,000 square feet. With the help of good friends, funds were approved, and we prepared construction drawings. The contrac-

Culture and entertainment are shared in a beautiful environment.

tor, Robert E. McKee, completed the building on schedule and within the budget. The workmanship was of the highest quality.

The final cost of the entire project, including theatrical equipment, furnishings, pipe organ, landscaping, and architect's fee, was under $3.5 million. With a construction cost of $17.80 per square foot it was the lowest-cost auditorium of its size in the country. Lincoln Center in New York, a smaller hall built at the same time, ran over $17 million.

At the opening concert, Eugene Ormandy, conductor of the Philadelphia Symphony Orchestra, proclaimed, "How I envy the Phoenix Symphony orchestra who can rehearse and play in Gammage." "The magical sounds of Gammage still haunt my ears," said Sir John Barbirolli of the Houston Symphony Orchestra, and George Szell of the Cleveland Symphony Orchestra said, "Probably the greatest hall of the twentieth century." "With acoustics like this, who needs a voice," declared Birgit Nilson, soprano with the Metropolitan Opera.

The remarkable acoustics are a result of the shape of the hall combined with appropriate reflective and absorptive surfaces. No wall is parallel to another wall, no ceiling surface parallel to the floor. All surfaces are convex so that sound is diffused and echoes

Every detail is an integral part of the whole design.

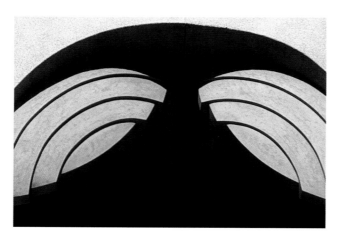

The hall was the lowest-cost auditorium of its size ever built in the U.S.

are prevented. The two "floating" balconies have open space behind, so that sound flows around them. Vern Knudsen was the acoustical consultant.

In order to facilitate the change from music to a drama setting, we had an innovative idea—the world's first telescopic steel orchestra shell. Engineered by George Izenour, at the touch of a button it converts the space from a concert hall to a drama theater in just twenty minutes. Knudsen and Izenour became an integral part of our theater design team and were instrumental to our success in this field.

The hall pioneered the cantilevered seat, which allows for easy cleaning. The continental-style seating eliminates radial aisles and allows the entire audience to exit in a few minutes. The sightline from every seat is perfect.

The color scheme was created by Mrs. Wright and was inspired by the earth tones of the Grand Canyon. When the Gammage Auditorium opened in 1964, the Phoenix Symphony had no place to perform except a high school auditorium. When they performed in Gammage, it was as though we were hearing their music for the first time. It is no exaggeration to say that the auditorium was instrumental in bringing culture to the Valley of the Sun. Over the years it has attracted the world's most talented artists and continues to sell out for almost every event.

David Dodge has recently designed a storage pocket so that the telescopic shell can be completely removed from the stage area. The stage will now more easily accommodate Broadway shows and musicals.

Praise from audience, performers, and critics brought world-wide fame.

The hall is the pride of the people of Sarasota.

VAN WEZEL PERFORMING ARTS CENTER

Sarasota, Florida
Date Completed: 1969
William Wesley Peters, Architect

One of the very few municipal theater-auditoriums in the country to operate at a profit, the building was described by the city manager, Ken Thompson: "The facility performs in a great manner, as measured by the enthusiastic responses from audiences who have sat in the near-perfect environment for maximum communication between artist and audience."

In the late sixties, George Izenour was asked by the city of Sarasota to help them realize their dreams for a

The folded plane roof is both structural and aesthetic.

Organic architecture favors the reflex over the major-minor axis.

community-oriented performing arts center to be located on the waterfront of Sarasota Bay. Their budget was unusually tight—$2.2 million for a 1,760-seat multi-purpose hall including furnishings, theater equipment, and site development. They required a hall that would serve a full spectrum of presentations—musical concerts, recitals, opera, ballet, and drama.

The design is striking, functional, and economical. On the beach the architect found a lovely seashell. The fluted pattern and soft lavender color inspired the design. The roof is constructed of folded plates of laminated plywood. The corrugations of the roof serve as

the structural system, an example of the integration of form and structure. The inspiration of the seashell is clear in the executed design.

Multipurpose use is achieved by a hydraulic stage. A moveable orchestra shell, together with provisions for adjusting the reverberation period of the hall, provides the utmost flexibility for different types of events. Two automated dividing curtains, visually opaque but acoustically transparent, allow a reduction in seating capacity to render ideal viewing and hearing conditions. "Sarasota theater-goers are high in their praise of the hall," said the critics on opening

Left: *The Lobby is a place for social interaction and art exhibitions.*

Below: *The plan is shaped to provide good sightlines, clear acoustics, easy audience circulation.*

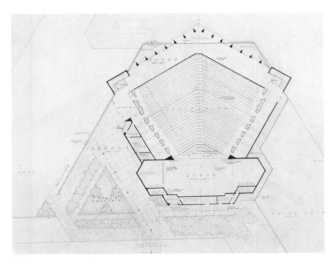

night." The show was *Fiddler On The Roof*, and it shared acclaim with the building: "Splendor of hall steals show at gala opening."

After twenty-eight years of successful operation, Taliesin Architects has been engaged to substantially enlarge and renovate the hall. To meet the needs of modern musical theater presentations, the stage will be expanded and a new orchestra shell installed, together with the latest technical equipment. The seating capacity will be increased to 2,400. With the increase in size of the lobbies and other facilities, the total area of the hall will be doubled.

RUTH ECKERD HALL

Clearwater, Florida
Date Completed: 1984
William Wesley Peters, Architect

The success of the Van Wezel Performing Arts Center brought us another theater-auditorium in Florida, this one a multi-purpose hall in the City of Clearwater. Like all Taliesin-designed theaters, it has continental seating with no center or radial aisles. This configuration brings the audience closer to the performers and affords ideal views from every seat.

There are 2,180 seats on one sloping floor, with the most remote seat less than one hundred feet from the stage. Both audience and performers have commented on the sense of intimacy of the Hall, remarkable for a space that seats this many people.

More than any other type of building, performing arts centers are subject to intense criticism—from the public, the performers, the professional critics, the technicians, the management, even the custodial staff. All become our judges.

"The acoustics are the best of any modern hall," said guitarist Carlos Montoya. Pianists Ferrante and Teicher wrote: "A beautiful hall, but more importantly, tremendous acoustics. It's a joy to play here." "Every sound, from the softest pianissimo to the loudest passage could be heard by the musicians themselves. It was love at first sound, an extraordinary experience," exclaimed Maestro Irwin Hoffman

Quality of design comes from using simple materials in a natural way.

Art teams up with technology

Right: *Grammar is the space relationship between the various elements.*

Bottom: *Form and function are one.*

at the first rehearsal of the Florida Gulf Coast Symphony Orchestra. "Ruth Eckerd Hall is a smashing success, a splendid concert hall with excellent visual and acoustic properties," said the critics.

The versatility of the hall allows a wide range of performances, from concert, opera, dance, musicals, drama, and lectures. The hall can be subdivided into a smaller 750-seat theater, perfect for drama.

The building has a diversity of uses. A community room seating 400 people provides space for banquets, receptions, recitals, community meetings, and special programs. There are several smaller meeting rooms. The spacious lobbies serve as exhibition galleries for paintings and sculpture.

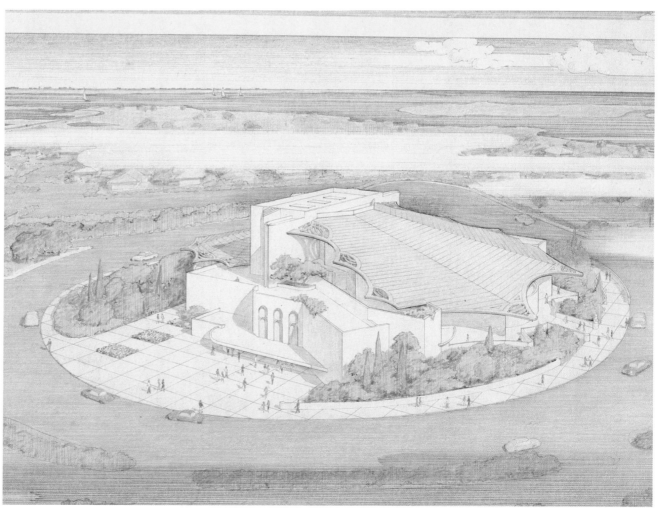

CENTRE COLLEGE FINE ARTS CENTER

Danville, Kentucky
Date Completed: 1973
William Wesley Peters, Architect

Dr. Thomas A. Spragens, president of Centre College, asked us to design a Fine Arts Center for the College of Liberal Arts and Sciences. Besides serving the needs of education, the facility has made a signif-icant contribution to the cultural life of the community, becoming the regional center for performing arts, especially opera, and drawing an audience from four adjacent states.

The center has three components, each serving a different aspect of the fine arts. Newlin Hall is a multipurpose theater-auditorium seating 1,483 persons. The Orchestra level seats 290, the Grand Tier has 1,193 seats. The advantage of this configuration is that the Orchestra level can function as an intimate recital hall or drama theater, easily closed off from the Grand Tier by a mechanically controlled traverse cur-

Operationally practical, artistically excellent, economically realistic.

An experimental theater, seating 330, provides a flexible facility for creative drama. Arena staging is accomplished by three moveable banks of seats that are operated by pneumatic casters. An overhead modular track system allows imaginative arrangements of the stage space. Almost any conceivable performance can be presented because staging is limited only by the imagination of its users.

Classrooms and studios are provided for teaching painting, drawing, graphics, and sculpture. An exhibition gallery shows art on loan from national museums.

The comments of performers, audience and critics were favorable. "How fascinating to find in Danville such a splendid concert hall with such wonderful acoustics." "One of the most beautiful halls I have ever seen, the acoustics are superb," said Isaac Karabetchevsky, director of the Symphony Orchestra of Brazil. Vivian Blaine affirmed, "An actor's privilege to perform in this theater." United Press International noted, "It attracts the best performers, regional, national and international."

tain. For musical events, an orchestra shell couples the stage with the house. When the shell is retracted, the stage serves drama, opera, dance, and musical comedy. A hydraulic lift platform extends the stage or serves as an orchestra pit for seventy musicians. Concealed power-operated acoustical curtains change the acoustics of the hall to respond to music or drama. Dressing rooms, drama rehearsal and music practice rooms are located on a lower level.

The lobby also serves as an art gallery.

BARTLESVILLE PERFORMING ARTS CENTER

Bartlesville, Oklahoma
Date Completed: 1982
William Wesley Peters, Architect

Writing for *Theatre Design and Technology*, William Allison commented: "The planning of a performing arts facility is, for most architects, a rare or unique experience. The subtleties of aesthetically critical space relationships, the complex technology, the sensitive interpersonal professional dependencies, the unremitting demands for ultimate conditions of sensory perception—all make such a project one of the most demanding an architect ever encounters. Too often the architect approaches that responsibility without specialized qualifying experience. Taliesin Architects qualify for our attention, both from individual capabilities and from long-continued teamwork on many performing arts projects."

A building for the performing arts is a good-time place, so it should have about it a sense of fun. Like good music and drama, the building itself should convey a spirit of both excitement and tranquillity. To achieve this requires an integration of innovative design with practicality and technology, visual and acoustic excellence, public comfort, and ease of access and egress. When sound and light, music and color combine harmoniously, they exert a magical quality and uplift the human spirit.

The multipurpose civic theater-auditorium for

Far left: *The character of the design identifies this as a place of entertainment.*

Left: *A performing arts center is an amalgam of technology, aesthetics, and common sense.*

Far right: *Architecture based on principles constantly searches for fresh forms.*

Below: *Space is a continuum and needs free expression.*

Bartlesville seats 1,800 people in a continental configuration, providing excellent sightlines. By electro-mechanical means, the physical and acoustical conformation of the stage and auditorium can be adjusted to provide an optimum environment for a variety of types of performing arts. These include concert, opera, musical theater, string and chamber orchestra, dance, drama, and lecture.

A flexible recital and rehearsal hall accommodates music, dance, and theater for an audience of 250 people. A community hall is used as an exhibition gallery, for trade shows, flower shows, formal balls, conventions and banquets for 500 persons.

"We haven't had to go looking for shows—they've been calling us," said managing director, Gary Moore. "The acoustics are outstanding. You can stand on the stage and converse with someone in the back of the hall in a normal voice," said critic Tim Wood.

HOSPITALITY AND RECREATIONAL

Terrace Court at the Arizona Biltmore Hotel—109 deluxe suites around an enclosed garden court and swimming pool.

Hospitality is another area where our personal experience gives depth to our design ability. The essential quality of the hospitality industry is being a good host to your guests. We have acquired a special understanding of the meaning of hospitality. At Taliesin, we are hosts to over 100,000 visitors a year. Our residential community has many house-guests, for whom we cook, serve meals, clean apartments, make beds, and entertain.

Hotels are classified into several different types. Many provide a wide range of services, but in general, hoteliers want the same things. They want their hotel to be so inviting and the experience so good, so memorable, that guests will want to return. A satisfied guest will spread the word about their good experience. Management wants an outstanding design that incorporates efficient operations and supports the success and profitability of their project. This is a very competitive industry, and in order to provide the highest level of service, a hotel or restaurant needs to be highly functional.

Designing a hotel is one of the most exciting things that an architect can do. A hotel is a world in itself. It includes a wide diversity of activities—sleeping, dining, recreation, entertainment, shopping, and conferences.

The Clubhouse in Manila, the Philippines.

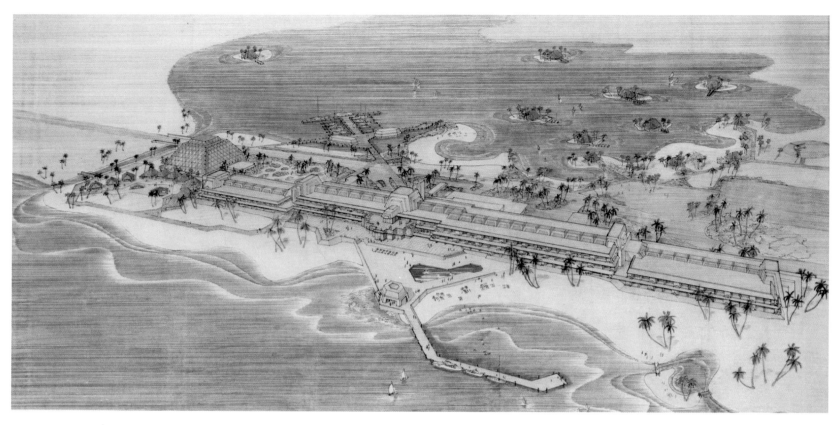

Design for the 240-room Reef Colony Resort on Ambergris Caye in the Caribbean.

Business, leisure, and social activities are part of the mix. A hotel is often host to people from other parts of the world. It is also a host in another sense, since it is frequently the place that represents the standard of quality of an entire community to out-of-town guests.

Our goal in hospitality design is to create a sense of luxury without depending on extravagant materials. The goal of a hotel is to provide good service. As architects, we can support the hotel staff in making their guests feel pampered. A good hotel will make the guests feel that they have a home away from home.

The Plaza Hotel in New York established a policy called "Everybody sells the strawberries." Years ago, they received a large shipment of delicious strawberries. The manager called the entire staff together and asked them to tell the guests. Bellboys, elevator operators, maids, clerks, doormen—everybody in the hotel would become a salesperson. The idea was a tremendous success, and they sold much more than strawberries. The architect's job is to create a hotel that the entire staff loves to work in so much that their enthusiasm spreads to their guests.

As more and more people today are placed in sedentary jobs, we are becoming increasingly aware of the importance of exercise as a part of physical fitness. More of our free time is devoted to recreational activities which often involve the whole family.

The clubhouses, ski lodges, and other recreational facilities that we have designed, while having some specialized functional requirements, all share one consideration: they are places for people. The spirit of their design is to provide an environment where people can relax, have fun, connect with each other, and get in touch with nature.

Designing architecture for hospitality and recreation is an opportunity to create an environment that provides people with a moment to be refreshed, to reflect, to reunite, and to re-create themselves.

Left: *Chula Vista Lodge in the Wisconsin Dells—interior view of the atrium.*

Below: *Design for the 300-room Vines Resort in Western Autralia.*

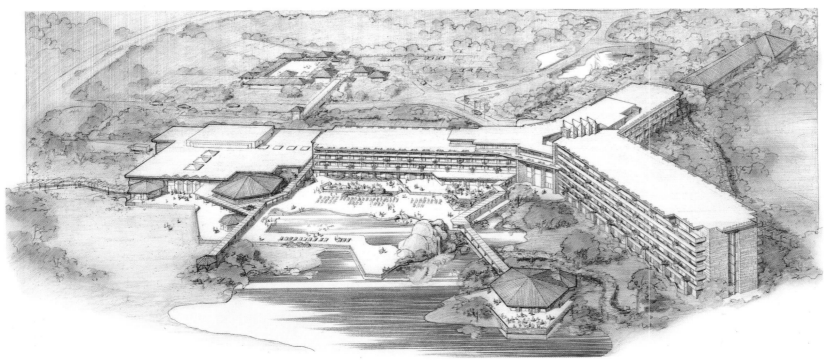

The Jewel of the Desert—a place to be refreshed and reconnected to life.

ARIZONA BILTMORE HOTEL EXPANSION

Phoenix, Arizona
Date Completed: 1987
John Rattenbury, Architect

Our initiation into working with the hospitality industry was sudden and intense. On June 20, 1973, the Frank Lloyd Wright-designed Arizona Biltmore Hotel caught on fire. Fortunately, it was unoccupied. In those days the Biltmore, like many desert resorts, closed for the summer months.

At the time of the six-alarm fire, the hotel was owned by Talley Industries. The company had purchased it from Phil Wrigley only two weeks before. When the smoke cleared, the devastation was obvious. The roof and top floor were gutted, the floors below in ruin. Taliesin Architects was asked if we could restore the hotel in time for a Price Waterhouse convention, which was booked for September 29, just eighty-one days away.

Working closely with the J. R. Porter Construction Company, we fulfilled our commitment. The roof was removed, reframed, and a new copper roof installed. Ceilings and walls were replaced, entirely new plumbing, air conditioning, and electrical sys-

The architectural experience is memorable—it brings the guests back.

*The entrance sculpture
starts the theme.*

tems installed. It took over one thousand workmen to complete this job, working twenty-four-hour shifts for the entire eighty-one days.

Virtually the entire firm of Taliesin Architects participated. We moved into the cottages at the back of the hotel. There were no useful drawings of the hotel and we had to start from scratch. We produced construction drawings for the contractor just minutes ahead of the crews who were pouring concrete and installing framing.

The scope of this incredibly fast-track project may be appreciated by just one statistic—after new air conditioning ducts and electrical systems were installed in the lobby, dining room and cocktail lounge, the ceilings were re-plastered, then gilded with 376,000 sheets of gold leaf, each skillfully applied and carefully hand-burnished. We combed the country for the few artisans still alive who were skilled in this special work. Many of them had long since retired. They climbed up on rolling scaffolds and worked long hours, finishing the backbreaking task on schedule.

We custom-designed new Axminster wool carpets for all the public area. Woven in Ireland, they were flown to Phoenix a few days before the deadline. The hotel reopened right on schedule, with every trace of the fire gone and every inch of every room completely refurbished.

Over the next seventeen years, we designed the Paradise Wing, the Valley Wing and Terrace Court, adding 400 rooms. We designed a conference center, a restaurant, and a fitness center. Every five years we completely refurbished the guestrooms and public spaces. Throughout this period, the Biltmore received the Mobil Five-Star award every year.

As the hotel ownership passed from Talley to the Rostland Corporation, we continued to design additions and improvements. The hotel opened year-round, and construction had to be done so as not to disturb the guests. Working with the contractor, we devised innovative methods of fabricating the concrete blocks and special construction techniques.

*The Orangerie—the beauty of the
room enhances the excellent cuisine.*

Virtually every detail in the hotel—carpets, furniture, light fixtures, logo and graphics, and chinaware, were custom designed by Taliesin artists, including Kay Rattenbury, John Hill, Cornelia Brierly, and Heloise Christa.

During the years that we were engaged at the Arizona Biltmore, we worked with many different hotel owners, managers, staff, contractors, and subcontractors. The contractors, M.M. Sundt Construction Co. and Kitchell Contractors invented some remarkably innovative construction techniques that reduced labor and expedited construction time.

Some years ago the hotel passed to new ownership and the interiors are now quite different.

Right: *The Gold Room —windows embellished with a touch of translucent color.*

Below: *Terrace Court is a hotel within a hotel.*

EL TOHONO CONFERENCE CENTER

Carefree, Arizona
Date Completed: 1995
John Rattenbury, Architect

Making improvements to an existing hotel is a challenge because everything must be done with minimum disturbance to the guests and under compressed time schedules. Another Five-Star property that we worked on was the Boulders Resort, owned and operated by Carefree Resorts. Our first task was a minor one, revamping the Women's Locker Room at the Golf Clubhouse. This led us to designing a new Spa and Fitness Center.

We did some interior design for the dining room and eventually added a new facility, the Tohono Conference Center. Tohono is a part of the El Pedregal Festival Marketplace, home to a group of exclusive shops and a 300-seat outdoor amphitheater. We were careful to blend our large addition into the existing buildings at El Pedregal. Attention was paid to function, flexibility, acoustics, lighting, and environmental systems. Although the purpose of the building is commercial, the design is humanized through its curved shapes, sense of scale, and warm desert colors and tex-

Inspiration for the design came from the giant boulders on the site.

*The design theme is
reflected in the details.*

tures. The wood doors in the conference center are inlaid with designs in copper, abstractions of the massive granite boulders on the site.

The main ballroom of Tohono seats 550 and can be subdivided into four meeting rooms. A full banquet kitchen serves the facility. A special feature is a 3,200-square-foot lobby/prefunction area, which has a retractable glass wall that opens onto an outdoor terrace. Adobe fireplaces and banco seating make this a delightful place to enjoy cocktails and views of the natural mountain boulders and desert sunsets. The prefunction area also serves as an art gallery. A business center includes administrative services for guests, such as cellular phones, fax, and computers.

The lower level of El Tohono is a branch of the Heard Museum, internationally known for its collection of Native American art.

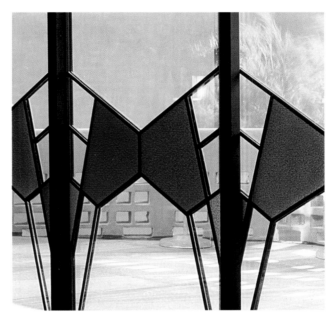

Left: *The abstract design inlay serves to protect the door from damage.*

Below: *The boardroom —understated elegance.*

*Warm and inviting spaces encourage
guests to return to this resort.*

THE SPRINGS RESORT

Spring Green, Wisconsin
Date Completed: 1997
Charles Montooth, Architect

A few miles from Taliesin lies a quiet green valley that is hidden from the rest of the world. A *Brigadoon* setting, it is an ideal location for a rural retreat. Executives and families escape from Chicago, Milwaukee, Madison, and the Twin Cities to discover its magic. The rolling hills are thick with oak, birch, and maple, and in spots where the rich earth has washed away, a golden-color sandstone is revealed. In the fall, the green colors pass into myriad shades of rust, gold, and amber.

Nestled along a bluff at the side of this valley, the resort hotel overlooks a 27-hole golf course. To soften the impact, the four stories are stepped back as they rise, carefully fit into the contours of the landscape. Because of the terraced design, golfers are not confronted with the impact of a large structure.

There are eighty luxury suites, each with a view ter-

The resort has its own private valley, forest, and golf course.

race that looks over the golf course to the wooded hills. A full range of amenities is included—restaurant, bar and grille, conference facilities, an indoor swimming pool, spa and sauna, a fitness center. A clubhouse and pro shop serve the golf course. Nearby are fourplex cottages. Guests are at first surprised to find such an elegant destination resort much closer than Hawaii or the Caribbean.

Native sandstone and limestone walls are laid up in horizontal bands, emulating the way the stone is found in the quarry. Shapes, colors, and textures are all designed to blend with the natural charm of the site, an example of mankind in harmony, rather than in competition, with nature.

The clubhouse—colors and textures blend with the natural charm of the site.

HARBORTOWN INN

Ventura, California
Date Completed: 1984
John Rattenbury, Architect

Ventura Harbor, located north of Los Angeles, consists of 164 acres of land and 124 acres of water. The

harbor has slips for several thousand boats. Waterfront property is scarce in Southern California, and the Coastal Commission puts severe restrictions on building near the water. There are very few hotels on the West Coast located right on the ocean, so this property is exceptional.

Harbortown Inn is the vision of entrepreneur-developers John Anderson and Fred Boulineau. The 250-room resort hotel, occupying twenty acres, is set

Gardens and interior courts provide shelter from the ocean winds.

Above: *Romantic architecture is architecture of the spirit.*

Right: *Harbortown Point is a time-share village surrounded by water.*

inside the harbor itself, virtually surrounded by boats. Every room has a private balcony or patio with a view of the marina, and is designed to capture the romance and excitement of waterfront activity.

The hotel consists of three separate parts. Guest registration occurs at the main hotel and conference center. There are three floors of guestrooms. Amenities include a coffee shop, swimming, hot tub, tennis, and gardens.

On an adjacent parcel, connected to the main hotel by a pedestrian bridge, is a "boatel." The boatel has forty-four boat slips so that guests can moor their boats overnight. It provides guest accommodations for the two hundred live-aboard families in the marina as well as for yachtsmen who keep their boats in the harbor. The building includes a seafood restaurant and

The main hotel and conference center.

Poolariums are intimate whirlpool spas set in flower gardens.

The hotel captures the romance and excitement of the harbor.

Seafood Anderson's restaurant is tiered so that everyone has a waterfront view.

cocktail lounge, with forty-four guestrooms above.

The third part, Harbortown Point, is located on a nearby part of the harbor. It consists of sixty-seven time-share suites, each with a fireplace, sitting room, and wet bar. Each suite has balconies with a glass windshield, which provides protection from the ocean winds.

An innovative feature at Harbortown Inn are the whirlpool spas, called Poolariums. Surrounded by flower gardens, these glass-domed structures are open at the top and have glass side panels that close when the weather is cool. The Poolariums serve as a conservatory for orchids and other tropical plants.

Guest room balconies overlook the marina and 2,000 boats.

Architecture is structure inextricably
related to time, place, and humankind.

WAIKAPU VALLEY COUNTRY CLUB

Maui, Hawaii
Date Completed: 1994
John Rattenbury, Architect

The Waikapu Valley Country Club nestles comfortably into its site in the foothills of the west Maui mountains. Its dome roofs blend with the rolling hills and bunkers of the championship golf course. The colors and textures of the building blend into the terrain. An adaptation of an unbuilt Wright design, the clubhouse was constructed fifty years after the design was first conceived.

The developers, Pundy Yokouchi and Howard Hamamoto, asked us for an original Wright design, so we searched our archives. In the forties, Wright

Sympathetic to its natural environment—the domes echo the golf course bunkers and rolling hills.

125

The building conveys a sense of welcome.

had designed a magnificent home for Fort Worth, Texas. It was not built, so he later adapted the design for an estate home in Acapulco Bay, Mexico. It too, was never built. In 1957, when Marilyn Monroe and Arthur Miller asked him to design their home in Connecticut, he adapted the concept once again, but it was destined to remain on paper.

The Waikapu Clubhouse is a synthesis of these three generic designs. The building has 68,000 square feet of space, much more than the original residential design. To preserve the design proportions, we put two thirds of the structure below ground. The lobby, pro shop, meeting rooms, dining room, and kitchen are on the upper level. The men's and women's locker rooms, Japanese furo, golf cart storage and maintenance are all located out of sight, below grade.

The roof of the main dining room is a 100-foot-diameter dome with a 25-foot-diameter skylight in the

Left: *The Lobby features an eight foot diameter art glass ceiling panel.*

Below: *The quality of organic architecture is dynamic, not static.*

center. The underside of this skylight is an inverted dome made of concentric rings of 1½-inch-diameter Plexiglas tubing. Around this are concentric wood boards laid over acoustic insulation.

Broad terraces extend out to capture the panoramic views. Across the isthmus of Maui lies the great extinct volcano, Haleakala. The crater emerges from the wreath of clouds that usually surrounds it. This extraordinary vista is framed on either side by the blue waters of the Pacific. With a mountain behind and green golf courses in front, the clubhouse has an idyllic setting. Constructed to the highest levels of quality by the Hawaiian Dredging Construction Company, it was awarded the Hawaiian Cement Achievement Award for design distinction and the innovative use of concrete.

COMMERCIAL

Seventh Day Adventist offices in Scottsdale, Arizona.

A building for commercial use, be it an office, bank, store, or manufacturing facility, must be eminently functional. It addition to its practicality, its design should provide an atmosphere that inspires those who work there. The structure also serves as an icon for its user, expressing the quality of the service or product that the company provides. It is physical evidence of the character of the company. In the case of a multi-tenant building, its design becomes an essential sales tool to attract new tenants and keep old ones.

Our goal in designing a building for commercial use is to create a facility that attracts clients and consumers and, at the same time, creates a better place for the employees to work. The productivity of employees

Design for Bush Services Office Building in St. Paul, Minnesota.

129

Above: *Blood Services Offices in Phoenix, Arizona.*

Right: *Blood Services Offices—the translucent sunshade controls heat and light.*

is directly linked to profits, and a healthy, effective, and beautiful environment is vital to efficiency. The quality of the workplace, in other words, is worthy of a thoughtful investment by the company that uses it, since it critically affects morale and output. This is as true for a factory as it is for an office.

The commercial buildings that we have designed, while varying greatly in form, size, and detail, have one thing in common—the quality of humanity in their design. In an age of blank glass walls, stainless steel, and high technology, we feel it is more important than ever that the workplace nurture our essential human qualities. This we do through the sensitive use of materials, textures, and warm colors, through balanced daylight and artificial light, and through consideration for human scale.

More and more people now have a computer at their workstation. This piece of equipment changes the way that we think about the working environment, especially with regard to lighting and seating comfort.

As electronic technology advances, much of the workforce is finding ways to work at home. We can also now work in cars and on planes. Telephone, fax, voice mail, express delivery, teleconferencing, computers, and the Internet are changing the need for a daily commute to a downtown office.

LINCOLN TOWER AND LIBERTY NATIONAL BANK

Louisville, Kentucky
Date Completed: 1966
William Wesley Peters, Architect

When John Acree, president of the Lincoln Income Life Insurance Company, asked us to design an office building in Louisville, Kentucky, Wes Peters had an innovative idea. The sixteen-story structure would be an "upside-down" building; that is, it would be largely built from the top down. The principle behind this idea is that steel is strong in tension while concrete is strong in compression. Although all tall buildings utilize steel columns in compression, steel is actually much stronger in tension than compression. Witness a suspension bridge with relatively tiny cables spanning an enormous distance.

Lincoln Tower was constructed by first building a vertical core of reinforced concrete. The core was slip-formed, meaning the same form was re-used for each new floor. The core contained the elevators, stairs, and utilities. Steel trusses were cantilevered out from the core to form the framing for the fifteenth and sixteenth floors. Steel tension cables were then dropped to the ground from the floor perimeter. The steel framing for the fourteenth floor was fabricated on the ground and then the floor was pulled up into place and hung from the tension cables. The thirteenth floor followed, to be hung below the one above, and so forth. Framing the floors on the ground was easier than constructing them in the air, and the absence of interior columns provided the maximum amount of rentable space.

When the roof was in place and the elevators run-

The precast concrete grille provides solar control—it is both practical and aesthetic.

*The productivity of employees increases
when their environment is humane.*

ning, finish work started on the top floor. By the time the lower floors were being lifted into place, the upper floors were being rented. The structure was economical to build because the cables that hang eleven floors are far smaller than the steel columns of conventional construction, and the only footing needed is under the core.

The lacy-patterned, precast concrete curtain wall acts as a sunscreen, effectively shading the glass but permitting light in and views out. A restaurant at the roof level is serviced by an outdoor observation elevator that runs

at 500 feet per minute or cruises at 50 feet per minute.

The innovative and cost-effective design allowed for an accelerated construction schedule. Rental income received ahead of a normal schedule, together with cost savings from the reduced weight of steel, made the venture exceptionally profitable. At the base of the tower, a large reflecting pond and fountain doubles as a cooling tower for the air conditioning system. Adjoining the building is a bank-in-the-round, the Liberty National Bank, which was designed as part of the complex.

Above left: *The floors are hung from above—there are no exterior bearing walls, only screens.*

Above right: *Interior space is laid out with maximum flexibility, and daylight reaches every office.*

*Mirrored ceilings and columns provide views
of the automobiles from every direction.*

MERCEDES BENZ SHOWROOM

New York City
Date Completed: 1982
John DeKoven Hill and Cornelia Brierly,
Interior Designers

The high level of design, performance, and craftsmanship of European automobiles is legendary. The quality of this showroom on Park Avenue, which first sold the British Jaguar and then the German Mercedes Benz, matches the quality of these automobiles. The elegance of these fine automobiles is echoed in the glamorous and exciting atmosphere of the showroom.

Automobiles are displayed on a turntable, and customers can ascend a ramp to view them from a higher angle. A circular mirror above the turntable provides birds-eye views so that every aspect of the car can be appreciated. Mirrored columns expand the sense of interior space. They also create a variety of vignette images of the cars on display. Interior planting areas with green foliage soften the hard surfaces of mirrors and metal.

All the furnishings were custom designed by Taliesin Architects and the showroom appointments match the craftsmanship of the automobiles.

Organic means intrinsic, where the character of the design grows from its function.

A bank that provides the community with more than banking services.

THE BANK OF SPRING GREEN

Spring Green, Wisconsin
Date Completed: 1972
William Wesley Peters, Architect

Despite its small size, under 10,000 square feet, this bank has a spacious quality. Although the nature of its business is commercial, it establishes an image in the community as a friendly bank. The open and informal lobby is designed to accommodate community meetings during non-banking hours. Allowing the community to use the bank this way creates the best possible public relations. Multiple use of space is also a good way to save our planet's energy and resources.

A fireplace creates a warm and inviting ambience.

After banking hours the lobby is used as a neighborhood meeting space.

Behind the eight teller stations are five private offices. Bookkeeping and work areas are screened from the public area by a sound-absorbent partition. The lobby carpet is a soft, burnt-orange color. The fireplace creates a warm and inviting ambiance, especially welcome in the winters when the temperature often falls to sub-zero. The native limestone walls are laid up with some stones projecting out, similar to the way that it is found in local quarries. Stone masonry is contrasted with oak paneling. The windows are of precast concrete, integrally colored to blend with the limestone. Natural lighting in the

lobby comes from the continuous band of windows as well as a skylight. A lounge for the employees doubles as a board of directors room, and has its own fireplace.

The curved forms reinforce the feeling of warmth and comfort, relieving much of the traditional formality associated with banks in the past. The character of the design reflects friendliness and the stone walls provide a feeling of protection. Although most transactions today are electronic, the customers of this rural community still want to feel that they can trust the bank with their life-savings.

LEWIS AND ROCA
LAW OFFICES

Phoenix, Arizona
Date Completed: 1990
John Rattenbury, Architect
Kay Rattenbury, Interior Designer

Orme Lewis was our attorney and a long-time friend of Taliesin. A true gentleman, he appreciated fine art and owned an extensive collection of paintings. In the sixties, his practice had started to expand and he asked us to remodel his law offices. The firm continued to grow, and by 1970 was so large that they decided to move to the new First National Bank Building. By now they needed 40,000 square feet of space. Orme had several requests—he wanted to connect the two floors with a spiral staircase and he needed lots of wall space for his art collection. Recognizing the importance of his support staff, he wanted the secretaries to have an especially good workspace.

The reception lobby—a warm feeling of congeniality and quiet efficiency.

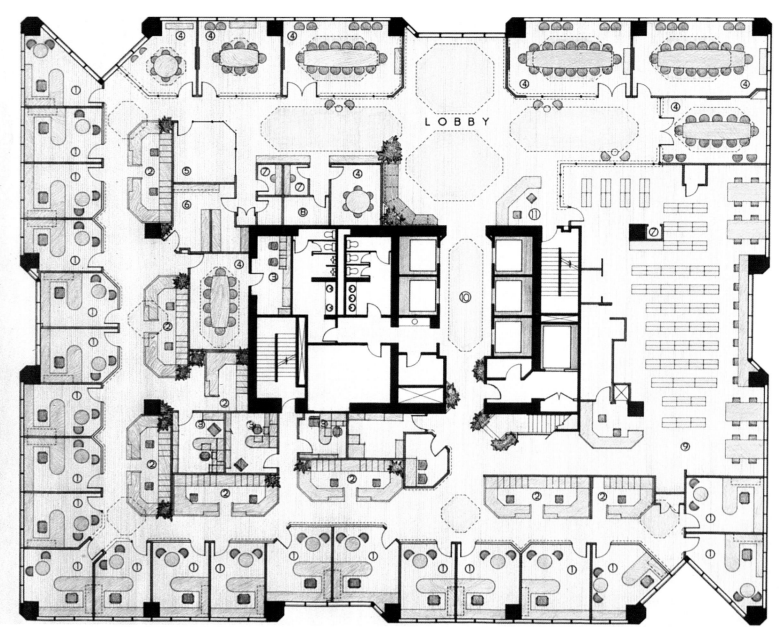

LOBBY

Typical floor plan—making the workspace both functional and friendly.

The firm practiced democracy. At their weekly meetings, young attorneys were encouraged to challenge older attorneys. To be a good lawyer, said Orme, you must not be afraid of either your opposing lawyer or the judge. He wanted this spirit of freedom to be reflected in the office layout. To achieve this, we put glass along the top of the interior partitions, expanding the sense of space and introducing natural light into the interior offices.

Over the years we continued to design additions to their office and in 1987, they moved once again, to Two Renaissance Square, a nearby hi-rise building. Once again we designed their offices. By now their need for space had grown to 116,000 square feet. To facilitate the

Conference rooms have windows and glass walls that transfer daylight to interior spaces.

traffic flow of lawyers, secretaries, and clients through the office space we removed all the square external corners. When people walk, they like to "cut corners," so we did this in the design, replacing each 90-degree corner with two 45-degree corners. We introduced natural daylighting to every office, utilized indirect artificial lighting, and custom designed all the cabinets, the lighting, the carpet, and much of the furniture.

Later we designed their offices in Tucson. In 1987 Cornelia Brierly designed the law office of Levy, Bivona and Cohen on Wall Street in New York.

Since lawyers deal so much with people who have painful problems and are in distress, we design law offices to have an atmosphere that is benevolent as well as efficient. Spaces are never imposing or intimidating, but full of light, with a warm and friendly ambience.

Conference room presentation board—design distinction in the smallest details.

WILLIAMS ELECTRONICS

Waukegan, Illinois
Date Completed: 1995
Lawrence W. Heiny, Architect
Elizabeth Rosensteel, Interior Designer

A well-lit, cheerful work-room promotes efficiency.

The commission to design the headquarters and manufacturing facilities for Williams Electronics afforded us an opportunity to demonstrate how architecture can directly affect the quality of the workplace. A leader in the design and manufacture of electronic games, chiefly pinball machines and casino gaming equipment, the company had plants and offices scattered throughout the Chicago area. For reasons of efficiency, they wished to consolidate their operations. They also wanted to provide an environment that would be inspirational to employees and customers.

Located in a heavily wooded, natural wetland preservation area, the first stage of the multiphase complex consists of an 185,000-square-foot structure, set back so as to be invisible from the highway. The parklike setting is a major determinant in the design of the structure. The reception lobby, administrative and sales offices,

The carpet design becomes integral to the architecture.

Above: *Industrial buildings can have distinction and still be affordable.*

Right: *The quality of a company's product or service exemplified by the quality of its architecture.*

and employees' break-rooms are located at the perimeter of the two-story building. Views through the tinted glass window-wall embrace trees and sky, bringing the beauty of nature directly into the workplace.

The floor plan is zoned so as to conceal service areas from the public and employee entrances. Parking for the 800 employees is interwoven with the trees so as to minimize the visual impact of automobiles.

An exposed aggregate finish on the precast concrete wall panels creates a soft texture that is in graceful harmony with the natural beauty of the site. Raked horizontal lines in the wall panels emphasize the quiet, horizontal character of the building. Careful attention to the design and quality of the interior furnishings and appointments was applied to line-workers' areas as well as staff areas, enhancing the concept that all are part of one team.

A relatively small investment in humanity and the quality of architecture enhances the spirit of the employees and pays off in terms of increased output.

The beauty of Nature comes to the workplace.

CIVIC

Marin County Civic Center,
San Rafael, California.

The purpose of government is to serve the people, and the character of a public edifice needs to convey a positive message about its form of government. In our republic, the spirit of freedom, fundamental to a democracy, is an essential attribute for a civic building. We strive to express this sense of freedom through the open space-flow of architecture. We also endeavor to express in civic architecture the ideals of public service—humanity, ethics, honesty, equal rights, and justice for all.

There was a time past when civic buildings were designed in monumental scale, presumably to impress on people the awesome power of government. Today, the character of a civic building more appropriately expresses the qualities of vision and leadership. As an icon for good leadership, a civic building needs to project an image that is both ideal-

Marin County Civic Center—the building that expresses the ideals of freedom, humanity and justice.

Above: *Design for the Truax Community Center—compatible with the residential neighborhood.*

Right: *The Denver Federal Center in Colorado—a plan to consolidate 27 government agencies.*

Marin County Civic Center—natural daylight fills the interior space.

istic and pragmatic. In computer language, it needs to be user-friendly.

The public and private sectors now recognize the advantage of supporting each other. Capital investment by government in urban architecture serves as a stimulus for investment by the private sector. To illustrate this, the Monona Terrace Convention Center in Madison, Wisconsin, resulted in over $50 million in new commercial buildings in the vicinity within a year.

This investment by the private sector provides an increase in tax revenues and an opportunity for the government to improve services.

We have completed twenty civic projects, for most of the different branches of government—Municipal, County, State, and Federal. Our experience in working with public officials is that they are fair-minded and responsible, eager to leave the world a better place than they found it.

Its curves are entrancing—there is always something to experience around the corner.

MONONA TERRACE

Madison, Wisconsin
Date Completed: 1997
Anthony Puttnam, Architect

Few cities in the world are blessed with such an enchanting circumstance of location as Madison, the capital city of Wisconsin. Situated between two lovely lakes, Mendota and Monona, it unfortunately took little advantage of its splendid views.

In 1938, Frank Lloyd Wright proposed a marriage between the city and Lake Monona. He envisioned a grand civic structure, half-circular in form, that would extend the city out into the lake. He presented his vision to Madison but it ran into political opposition, and would not be built in his lifetime. It would, in fact, take a journey of sixty years before his imaginative scheme was realized. On the way, the project had both champions and detractors. At long last the idea triumphed. In 1992, a feasibility study convinced the city that the center would generate sufficient revenues to justify its expense, a public referendum approved funding, and construction commenced.

Taliesin Architects headed the architecture/engineering team that took Wright's design concept and incorporated all the functional needs of a modern convention center. Built within the designated budget of $67.1 million, the building opened on schedule in July 1998. An instant and overwhelming success, it is booked years ahead and already generating

The Monona Terrace Conference and Convention Center—it gave inspiration to the community.

*For the first time people can really experience
the lovely lakes that surround Madison.*

Above: *The Madison Ballroom seats 1,000.*

Right: *The Grand Terrace allows for dining and other events on the lakeside.*

twice as much income as was predicted. Now beloved by the citizens, the center has created a great sense of civic pride. It is also pumping vitality into an urban redevelopment program for the City of Madison.

The 250,000-square-foot convention center includes an exhibition hall, ballrooms, meeting rooms, a community center and a theater/lecture hall. The public reception areas and lakeside lobbies provide space for exhibitions, receptions, cocktail parties, and dining. The roof garden level of the structure is sixty-five feet above the lake, which makes it even with the city street level at this point. Parking for 600 cars on four levels is located out of sight and the parking structure serves as a bridge over the highway and railway tracks that run between the city and the lake.

People walk directly from the city along a pedestrian mall onto a roof of the building, which is constructed as a garden park, a delightful place for relax-

ation, lake-views, picnics and evening concerts.

Dome-shaped fountains echo the dome of the state capitol, the most dominant architectural feature of Madison. But whereas the capital building imposes a sense of awe and power, Monona Terrace opens a friendly hand and invites people to enjoy the compa-

ny of each other on the shores of Lake Monona.

Executed almost two generations after it was designed, it is a testimonial to the timeless quality of organic architecture, to the wisdom of building in harmony with the environment, to humanity in architecture, and finally, to the power of the people.

Earth berms blend the building with the desert.

CENTRAL ARIZONA PROJECT HEADQUARTERS

Phoenix, Arizona
Date Completed: 1986
Anthony Puttnam, Architect

The arid deserts of southwest Arizona have the potential of becoming a garden paradise, but for this to happen, they need an essential ingredient—water. Water is essential to life in the land of the sun, where the annual rainfall is minimal and temperatures in the summer soar well over 100 degrees. Native plants use ingenious water management techniques to preserve this precious commodity and now mankind has learned to do the same.

The Central Arizona Project is responsible for managing an allotment of Colorado River water to the cities and agricultural districts of the south central part of the state. Water that originates in the Rocky Mountains is delivered through a system of

Computers control water distribution to the state of Arizona.

canals that stretch across Arizona for 336 miles. The 1.5 million acre-feet of water that they deliver every year are carefully measured and controlled by a computer system.

The U.S. Bureau of Reclamation required a 50,000-square-foot facility on an eighty-acre site. Their headquarters contain administrative and management staff as well as the maintenance department that keeps the canals in operation. In their position of providing a service to the public, the CAP wanted their facility to serve as a model for effective water conservation and sensitivity to the fragile desert ecology.

The building is designed not to intrude on but blend with the desert. The low profile of the single-story structure does not compete with the broad expanse of the landscape. The sloping exterior walls echo the forms of the surrounding mesa and colors

and textures match the desert. Earth berms around the base of these walls blend the structure into its site and also provide a natural insulation. The structure itself has a high level of thermal insulation. The landscaping around the building consists of indigenous plants that require no irrigation. The character of the building is a clear expression of its purpose.

Natural daylighting illuminates interior office spaces, providing quality light while reducing energy cost. A broad reflecting shelf below the continuous strip window bounces indirect sunlight up to the ceiling. Interior courtyards and light wells introduce light into the inner office areas, and generous roof overhangs in these locations block direct sunlight.

A sophisticated computer system monitors and carefully regulates the supply of water, otherwise known as "Arizona's gold."

MESA COMMUNITY CENTER

Mesa, Arizona
Date Completed: 1980
John Rattenbury, Architect

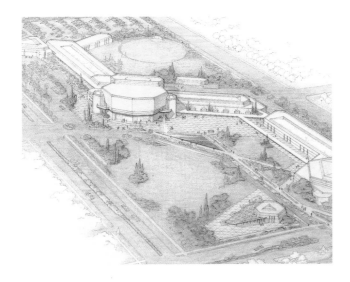

The City of Mesa is one of the fastest-growing cities in the Southwest, and when they announced their plans to build a Community Center, they received responses from architects all over the United States. The Center was to include an auditorium, a drama theater, an exhibition hall, a library, an art museum,

Left: *A civic auditorium, exhibition hall, library, senior center, art museum and amphitheater.*

Architecture is the welding of imagination and common sense.

Right: *The Mesa Amphitheater seats 2,000 for concerts, cultural and educational events.*

Below: *The Plaza, host to Arts and Craft shows, has an Arcade that provides shade from the sun.*

an amphitheater, and a senior center.

We were chosen to prepare a master plan for the twenty-three acre site. The first building to go up was Centennial Hall, a multipurpose building of 40,000 square feet. Although the budget was tight, we were able to create a great deal of flexibility in the way the building could be used without compromising on quality.

The hall hosts over one thousand events every year. It is used for a full range of social, cultural, commercial, and political events, ranging from assemblies and lectures to conventions, trade and community shows, exhibitions, musical concerts, and square dances. The main room seats 1,200 persons at banquets. Four smaller meeting rooms can be opened into each other and also into the main room. Energy conservation features of the design have kept fuel bills well below projected figures. Theatrical lighting and sound systems are supplemented by sub-floor and above-ceiling utilities.

Over the years, the Grand Plaza was added, creating a space for arts and crafts shows and other out-

door events. Protection from the sun is provided by a colonnade of cast concrete sculptural piers, and the hard surface of the Plaza is softened by several pools and fountains, scaled down so that they relate to the size of children.

An outdoor amphitheater seating several thousand people was constructed. This facility has been used for all kinds of events, ranging from lectures to communi-ty picnics and musical concerts. Later we added a center for senior citizens.

The ultimate judgement of how well a public building works lies with the people who operate it, the people who use it, and the people who regard it as a symbol of what the community stands for. The Mesa Community Center has stood the test of time and continues to effectively serve its citizens.

*Rocky Mountain National Park
headquarters, Estes Park, Colorado.*

ROCKY MOUNTAIN NATIONAL PARK HEADQUARTERS

Estes Park, Colorado
Date Completed: 1967
E. Thomas Casey, Architect

Rocky Mountain National Park is one of America's most famous and beautiful wilderness areas, welcoming many thousands of visitors every year. This building is its gateway. Set at the entrance to Estes Park, it serves as the Park Service administrative headquarters and visitor center, providing information to thousands of visitors who come every year. Hourly orientation programs in the 250-seat auditorium educate the public on the natural history of the Rocky Mountains. The structure serves a noble cause—park officials, through lectures, movies, and literature, inform the public and make them aware of the need to preserve and enhance our natural environment. The Park Service makes the auditorium available to the local townspeople for meetings during the time it is not being used by visitors.

Innovative construction techniques kept costs down.

Right: *The form and materials of the building blend with the forest and mountains.*

Below: *Informing the public of the need to preserve our natural environment.*

The design takes its inspiration from the scenic grandeur of the evergreen forest and its majestic mountain backdrop. Masonry walls were constructed of native sandstone using an innovative prefabrication technique. Instead of being built in place, the walls were cast as flat slabs on the ground nearby. Stones of different sizes and colors, taken from an old quarry, were laid with their flat surface down in flat beds of sand. Many of these stones were covered with a colorful lichen growth. Steel reinforcing bars were then set over the rocks and concrete was poured on top, creating a flat reinforced slab, or panel. After the concrete had cured, a crane tilted the panels vertically, exposing the bottom surface of rocks. The panels were then lifted into place and set with the rock surface exposed to the exterior.

The exterior trusses are constructed of a special type of steel called Corten. The natural rust coating of Corten weathers to become an impermeable finish, deep Sienna brown in color, sealing the steel against further rusting. No maintenance is required on the finished surface. The Corten trusses serve as structural supports for the roof and also carry a panoramic viewing balcony that wraps around the auditorium.

Structure and aesthetics are completely integrated in a design that echoes the abstract patterns of the forest and mountain forms. Seen in its setting of evergreen trees and rugged mountains, the building naturally and harmoniously blends with and complements the beauty of the landscape.

Structure and form integrated — the design is an abstraction of mountains and evergreens.

165

EDUCATIONAL

*Taliesin West, headquarters of Taliesin
Architects and the FLLW School of Architecture.*

What could be more important to the future of civilization than for humanity to constantly strive to raise the standard of education and make it available to every person on earth? Taliesin has an abiding interest in education, and every member of Taliesin Architects participates in the Frank Lloyd Wright School of Architecture. Our architectural firm is a teaching office, constantly revitalized by the influx of apprentices from all over the United States and overseas.

This daily involvement and personal, hands-on experience in education gives us a special insight when we design schools. We understand the needs of both the faculty and students who use the building. On our own campus we seek innovative ways that architecture can

Mettler Dance Studio, Tucson, Arizona.

Medical Clinic for Dr. Rorke.

support the learning process

Our designs for educational facilities recognize the importance that the environment has in edifying young people. Buildings can subtly support learning in ways beyond functionality. When we design a school, we seek to impart certain qualities of life to the students through the character of the architecture itself. At a time when violence in schools is increasing at an alarming rate, architecture can assist parents, teachers, and society to pass on real values to students. The qualities of organic architecture can be read as a code of human ethics—integrity, honesty, humanity, freedom, spiritual aspiration, harmony, beauty, the appreciation of nature, love of family, and honor of the individual. These are virtues in a human being, our heritage to young people, yet character development seems to be left out of most school curriculums.

Our commitment to education also benefits us as architects. One of the best motivations for continuing to learn is to undertake the responsibility of teaching. We have to work hard to stay ahead of the inquiring minds of our young apprentices.

THE PRAIRIE SCHOOL

Racine, Wisconsin
Date Completed: 1990
Charles Montooth, Architect

The idea for creating this co-educational country day school came some thirty-four years ago from Mr. and Mrs. Samuel C. Johnson. Pioneers of the idea, they continue to guide, inspire, and sponsor the development of the school. Starting with 170 pupils, over the years the Prairie School has grown to a current enrollment of over 600.

Construction started on a fast-track schedule and the first part of the campus was built in only eighty-seven days. As the school continued to grow every year, the faculty members were invited to participate in the planning process. Their input to the design is a major reason why the school functions so effectively.

Because of the need to accommodate constant growth, and also to keep everything in human scale, the plan of the campus is decentralized. Spaces are designed for flexibility and many interior walls are

The library—as pleasant a place for reading as one's own home.

*Smaller units foster a
close relationship between
teacher and student.*

*The scale of children
determines the propor-
tions of the design.*

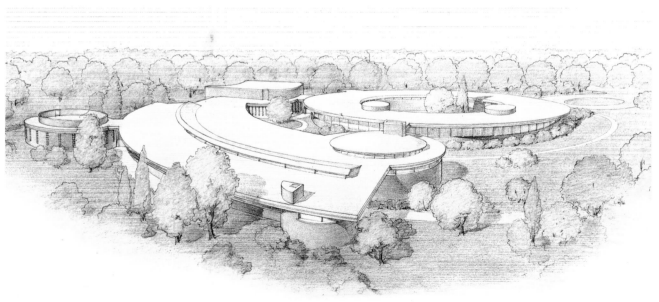

A school that teaches the young how to learn, rather than stuffing their memory.

built as demountable partitions. Lighting fixtures that provide both direct and indirect lighting are designed to be easily moved. An individualized learning center utilizes computers and educational hardware.

Organic principles were followed from the start and the architecture is kept in scale with the students, who range in age from pre-school through high school. The goal of the design is to nurture and inspire the students. Circular forms, brick masonry of a warm color and texture are combined with natural wood paneling, cabinets, and shelving to reinforce the humane aspects of the school.

The school provides a well-rounded education.

Facilities now include Lower, Middle and Upper Schools, a dining hall, a theater, a fieldhouse, a gymnasium, laboratories, and even a glass-blowing shop. Although many of the buildings have different forms because of their special uses, unity is achieved in the campus through simplicity of shapes and a minimal number of different materials and colors.

The campus is in harmony with its environment, and through the careful use of glass makes a friendly connection to the prairie landscape. The students learn responsibility and respect for humanity and nature. The school is not run for the students, it runs *with* them.

Arches are used in a fresh way, but still follow time-tested principles.

172

DAMAVAND COLLEGE

Mt. Damavand, Iran
Date Completed: 1978
William Wesley Peters, Architect

North of Teheran, under the shadow of the soaring peak of Mount Damavand, the twenty-acre campus of this women's college is a place where East meets West and both share their rich and varied cultural heritage. Ancient Persia made significant contributions to world culture, in literature, poetry, music, art, and architecture. The design of the campus follows the belief that the only safe tradition is principle.

The college is designed for an enrollment of 1,200 students with dormitories for 300. The educational goal of the college is to break the bonds of learning by rote. The liberal arts program is designed to develop the mental and spiritual powers of the individual and encourage independent thinking.

Traditionally, the Madresseh, or Persian school, was composed of buildings that surrounded a spacious garden courtyard. The plan of Damavand College follows

Iran was once part of ancient Sumeria, where brick and glazed tiles were used 30,000 years ago.

this concept in principle. The library, theater and lecture hall, cafeteria, and student center are located within the center of a compound ringed by classrooms, administrative offices, gymnasium, and swimming pool. The buildings follow the contours of the sloping site and are connected by a series of covered walkways. Brick masonry is

ideal for curved shapes, and the design integrates form and structure. Arched and vaulted roofs are covered with glazed turquoise tile. With an abundance of craftsmen available, the architecture makes full use of their talents.

The Persians were highly skilled in spanning space with brick arches, vaults, and domes, creating beauti- ful and enduring structures. These age-old techniques have been translated into a modern design that connects the rich heritage and culture of the past to the science and technology of today. The character of the buildings expresses their purpose and they are at home in the dramatic landscape.

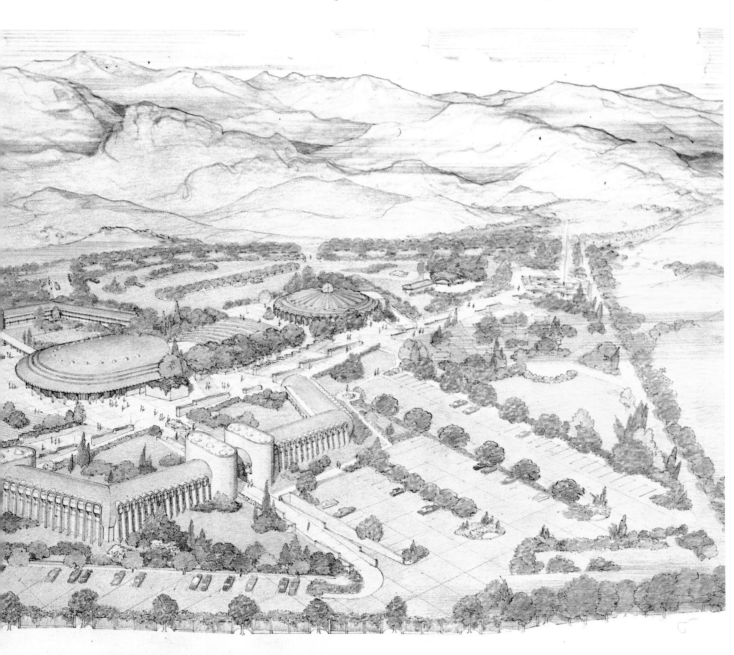

Far left: *Glazed tiles are part of the art and culture of Persia.*

Left: *The design was shaped by the cultural context, the program, and the nature of the site.*

ARIZONA STATE UNIVERSITY MUSIC SCHOOL

Tempe, Arizona
Date Completed: 1971
William Wesley Peters, Architect

As Arizona State University expanded, the school of music outgrew the space that we originally provided at the Gammage Auditorium. The first phase of the new Music School Building was a 100,000-square-foot structure containing faculty offices, administrative offices, classrooms, studios, and practice rooms for individuals.

Set in the center of the building is a 500-seat multipurpose theater and lecture hall, fully equipped for musical and dramatic productions. This theater is used frequently for small opera performances. On the top floor, a 130-seat theater serves for recitals and lectures. An outdoor amphitheater is also provided.

The circular shape of the building works well for

The 500-seat auditorium is used for opera productions, musicals, recitals, and drama.

The circular form of the ASU Music Building is a natural consequence of its function.

177

music practice rooms. Rooms that are rectangular in shape have parallel walls and these create undesirable echoes. The walls of the circular music school are naturally radial, not parallel, and this prevents "flutter echo." To stop sound transfer between rooms, the walls are designed for maximum sound isolation.

The exterior of the building is constructed of precast concrete panels, integrally colored. Used in combination with brick, it matches many of the buildings on campus.

CORBIN EDUCATIONAL CENTER

Wichita, Kansas
Date Completed: 1964
William Wesley Peters, Architect

When an institution breaks with traditional ways, it is usually because of the vision and courage of an individual. Wichita State University had such a person. Dean Jackson Powell was a quintessential teacher, and he had some advanced ideas on teacher education. He believed that the architectural environment of the classroom is an essential component of education. To bring inspiration to his campus, he looked to the creative abilities of Frank Lloyd Wright.

Following his preliminary design sketches, Taliesin Architects completed the first of the two buildings that were originally designated as the Juvenile Cultural Center.

Classrooms and administrative offices are grouped

The incessant force of gravity brings everything to a level plan—the line of repose.

At the center of the school is a sunlit garden court.

around an interior garden court to create a sense of open, sunlit space. A broad esplanade extends beside a pool and planting area. Outdoor, landscaped roof terraces extend into the split-level building. Workroom-studios are located on the mezzanine, and all classrooms and lecture halls receive natural daylight.

The stairways connecting upper and lower levels become belvederes that provide interesting views as one moves vertically through the space. Precast concrete, exposed aggregate panels contrast with glass to create a clean, simple, and harmonious ensemble.

Below: *Every detail echoes the design theme.*

THE FRANK LLOYD WRIGHT CENTER

Scottsdale, Arizona
Date completed: 1997
John Rattenbury, Architect

Taliesin West is designated as a National Historic Property. As the interest in Frank Lloyd Wright and organic architecture continues to grow, so does our need for more extensive visitor facilities. The new Frank Lloyd Wright Center, at the entrance to the 500 acres of Taliesin West, will be the first stop for all visitors. The facility is based on a design made by Wright for the Arizona desert.

The Center is capable of handling up to 250,000 visitors a year, more than twice the current number. An exhibition of photographs, models, dioramas, together with lectures and a multimedia show, describe the life, work, and ideas of Frank Lloyd Wright and the Taliesin Fellowship. It is based on the "In The Realm Of Ideas" exhibit that toured the U.S and other countries some years ago. A model Usonian house is part of the tour, allowing visitors to experience the interior space of a Wright home. There is a bookstore, gift shop, and the Taliesin Café.

Outdoor events, such as corporate meetings, conferences, banquets, weddings, and other business and social activities are held in the courtyard plaza. These evening events often include several hundred people at a cocktail party and catered dinner.

The Center serves other needs. It includes a new facility for the Frank Lloyd Wright Archives, which is responsible for preserving the life work of Frank Lloyd Wright—his designs, his philosophy, his writings, and his art collections. The Archives will have galleries, vaults, offices, and study facilities for scholars.

Seminar facilities will provide space for workshops, conferences, lectures, and symposiums. An architectural research and development facility will experiment with new materials, construction methods, and innovative ideas for architecture.

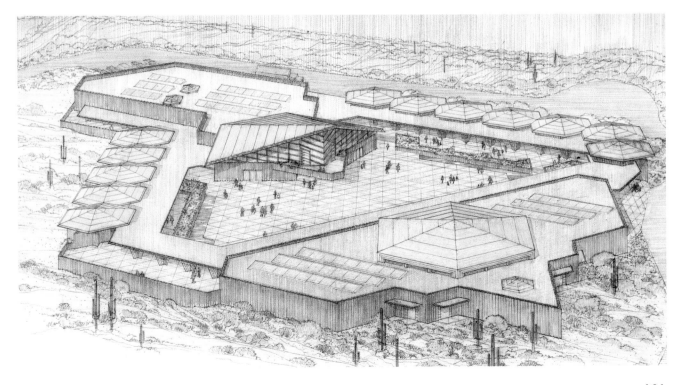

Responding to the ever-growing public interest in organic architecture and Frank Lloyd Wright.

Sun Health Alzheimer Center, Peoria, Arizona.

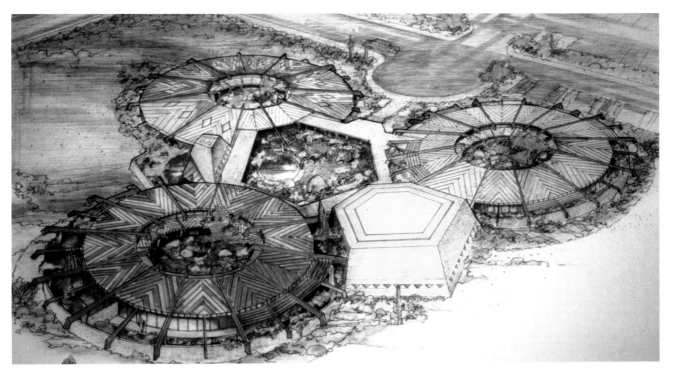

Scottsdale Institute for Health & Medicine, a center for natural healing and better health.

Our designs in the field of health care go far beyond the utilitarian. The scientific aspects of health care must certainly be addressed, with great respect for their complexities and constant improvements. But it is the other side of health care, the caring side, where organic architecture can provide significant support to the healing process. When architecture nurtures the human spirit, brings warmth, cheer, and optimism to the patient, it works in harmony with doctors, nurses, and modern medicine.

Now that conventional medical practice is starting to recognize and work together with natural healing methods to provide integrative medical services, organic architecture is more likely to have a chance to make a real contribution to health care. It can do this by supporting the process of maintaining good health and preventing illness, and by providing an environment that assists healing.

Good health and healing are ultimately the work of the human body, the mind, the heart, and the spirit. Drugs, surgery, and holistic methods only help the body to do its miraculous work. When a patient needs surgery, intensive care, or special treatment, architecture needs to be highly functional. During the much longer recuperative period, or for patients with long-term illnesses or disabilities, the situation is different. That is where architecture can be a partner to the healing process. About the only thing of beauty in most hospitals and clinics is the bouquet of flowers that a thoughtful friend or relative provides. By surrounding a person with the joy and serenity of a beautiful environment, appropriate and cheerful colors, music, optimistic lighting, and a view of nature, architecture can work in synergy with medicine and human care.

Organic architecture also makes a contribution to good health and the prevention of illness. Buildings themselves should be healthy, which means introducing sunlight, fresh air, and non-toxic materials. By feeding the human spirit with beauty, architecture nurtures better health.

Hospital patients should never be imbued with the idea that they are sick. Instead, health should be constantly before their eyes.

—FLLW

183

The architecture is a vital component of health care, influencing patients in a positive way.

CORINNE DOLAN
ALZHEIMER CENTER

Chardon, Ohio
Date Completed: 1993
Stephen Nemtin, Architect

What could be more challenging than the care of people with Alzheimer's disease? The illness is still a mystery and has, as yet, no cure. The anxiety, confusion, and helplessness of the patients require very special care. The facility that serves their needs must support their individuality but not patronize them; their humanity must be nurtured and their dignity preserved.

When we were asked to design this research-oriented experimental residence facility, there was no good model to follow. Patients were responding poorly to traditional institutions because they were inhuman, employing chemical restraints and locked doors.

Alzheimer symptoms include the loss of short-term

Forms, colors, textures, lighting—all designed to promote a sense of well-being.

Above: *The buildings are healthy, non-toxic, full of fresh air and sunlight.*

Right: *Patients are vulnerable—architecture should care for them, love and restore them.*

memory and an inability to concentrate. In order to understand the nature of the problem, Stephen Nemtin spent several days living with the patients and staff. The innovative design solution for a new center arose from a deep appreciation of the problem.

The fundamental idea of the design is that the environment itself is a vital component of health care and can influence patients in a positive way. The architecture of this center is humane in every aspect—scale, form, and materials are designed to encourage the well being of the patients and lessen their sense of frustration, agitation, and isolation. The design helps them feel relaxed, safe, independent, and functional. Rather than confine patients,

the facility is designed to allow them to wander freely. The open interior has an inviting atmosphere. Garden courts, lit with natural daylight, create a feeling of conviviality. Cooking, dining, and activity areas provide opportunities for participation and spontaneous social interaction. To assist patients who wander and cannot find their way back to their room, "cues" are provided. A glass-enclosed niche outside their room contains photos and mementos of loved ones. Since their long-term memory is still alive, they recognize this cue.

Materials are natural and simple: brick, wood, and stucco in warm, earth tones. Exterior terraces allow patients to enjoy the outdoors.

Nurturing better health by feeding the human spirit with beauty.

187

SUN HEALTH
ALZHEIMER CENTER

Peoria, Arizona
Date Completed: 1996
Stephen Nemtin, Architect

The compassionate architecture of this center is designed to help patients maintain a quality of life. The Sun Health Alzheimer Center consists of two buildings, a treatment center and a hospice. Sunlight is introduced to the interior of the building by clerestory windows or interior courtyards. The buildings are like a home, warm and inviting, friendly and optimistic.

Right: *Everything is designed to have a spirit of optimism.*

The building supports individuality and allows patients to preserve their dignity.

Patients are encouraged to roam, interact, and participate in life's activities.

The design comes from a deep appreciation of the nature of the problem.

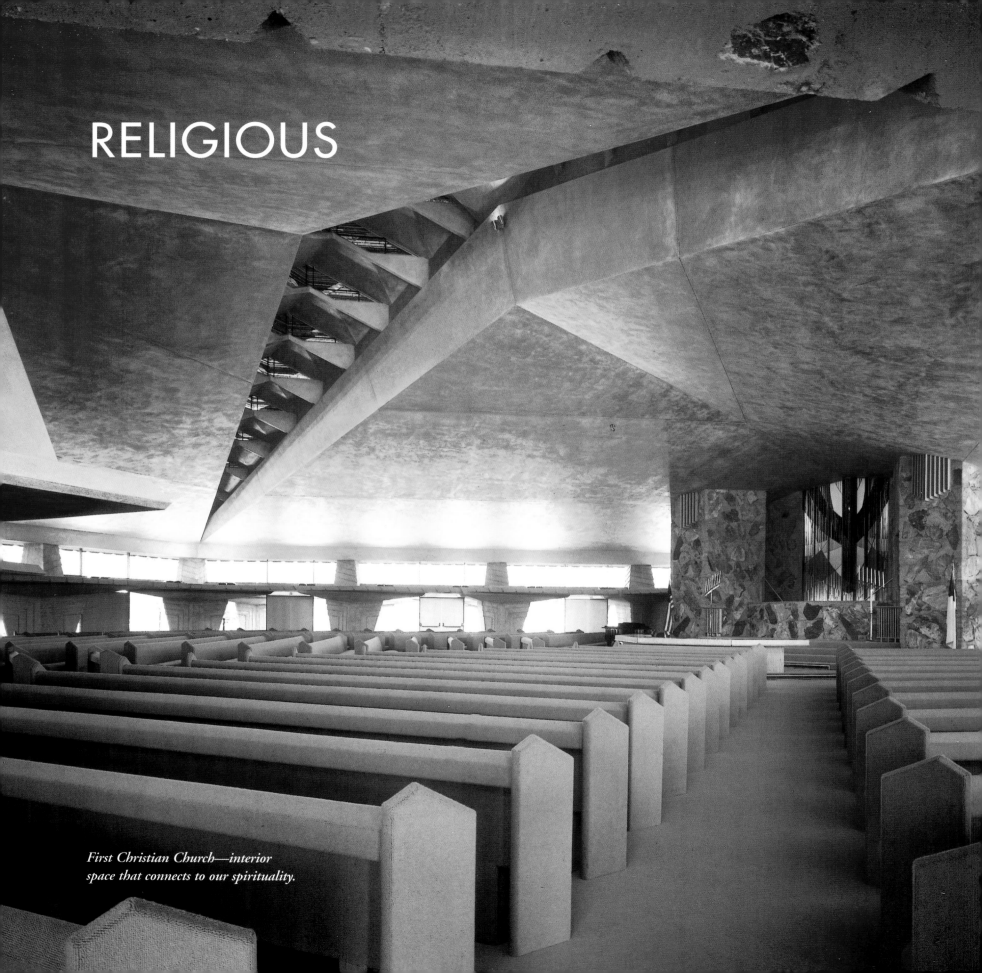

RELIGIOUS

*First Christian Church—interior
space that connects to our spirituality.*

As the gathering place for people of a religious faith, a church, temple, or synagogue is a building for prayer and the worship of God. Its purpose is to help us connect to the divinity within us, and its essential character is one of inspiration. It is appropriate, then, that it reflect something of the beauty of nature, since nature is the manifestation of God.

Architecture can be a powerful tool of communication in our pursuit of a higher ideal. It can touch the creative spirit that is within us, encourage us by lifting our hearts. A house of worship serves as a symbol, an abstract expression of the historic roots of a particular faith, its belief in immortality. Its symbolism may be expressed by its form and also by all its details.

Beth Sholom Synagogue, Elkins Park, Illinois—the symbol of Mount Sinai, a tower of light.

Desert Palms Presbyterian Church, Sun City West, Arizona.

The Annunciation Greek Orthodox Church, Wauwatosa, Wisconsin. The dome floats ethereally over the congregation in a modern expression of a Byzantine form.

At the time that Frank Lloyd Wright died, he was working on designs for the Annunciation Greek Church in Wauwatosa, Wisconsin, the Beth Sholom Synagogue in Elkins Park, Pennsylvania, and the Pilgrim Congregational Church in Redding, California.

Taliesin Architects prepared the construction drawings for each of these. For the Greek Church, we designed the pews, icon screen, altar, bishop's chair, and the vestments. Taliesin artist Gene Masselink painted the icons. For the Beth Sholom Synagogue, we

designed the pews, altar screen, rabbi and cantor's chairs, and menorah.

Commissioned some years later, the First Christian Church is based on a design that Wright made for the Southwest Christian Seminary.

In the religious buildings that we design, our goal is not to impress people with the awesome power of divinity but to connect them to their own spirituality. Architecture can inspire hope, compassion, and love. It can support the values by which our faith enlightens us. Materials that are inanimate come alive when shaped into beautiful forms. As the beauty of nature links us to our spirit within, so organic architecture can help unite us to our faith.

St. Mary's reflects the new spirit of the Catholic church.

ST. MARY'S CATHOLIC CHURCH

Alma, Michigan
Date Completed: 1970
William Wesley Peters, Architect

The message of the Catholic Church is one of faith, hope and love, and this is expressed in every aspect of the design of St. Mary's. Although the content of the message has not changed in almost two thousand years, some aspects of the service and the way that the church reaches out to its congregation have been mod-

Left: *Inanimate materials come alive when shaped into beautiful forms.*

Below: *The curved aisle is more humane than the traditional, straight center aisle.*

ernized. While embracing the people in a warm and friendly manner, this house of worship still preserves a sense of mystery and spirituality.

Its circular form creates an intimate atmosphere for the 700 parishioners. Amply spaced pews exit to gently sloping side aisles that converge on the Sanctuary. An S-shaped ramped aisle begins near the entry, passes the Baptistery chapel, and approaches the altar. The informality of the curved central aisle is more humane than the traditional straight center aisle that points right at the altar and cuts the congregation in half.

Curved masonry walls are shielded by earth berms that connect the building to the ground, and the graceful, wood-framed, conical roofs express the timeless spirit of aspiration. A stained glass skylight extends from the central spire to the smaller spire over the sanctuary. The sculpture of the Virgin Mary is by Taliesin Architects, as are all the designs for stained glass, sanctuary screens, and other appointments.

The rectory is connected to the church by a covered walkway and cloister that surrounds a garden court. Every detail works together to create an atmosphere of reverence and an experience that is inspirational and uplifting.

Below: *Love of beauty is reverence of God.*

Right: *The stained glass was designed as an integral part of the architecture.*

ASCENSION LUTHERAN CHURCH

Scottsdale, Arizona
Date Completed: 1964
William Wesley Peters, Architect

The plan of this church is based on the elemental geometric form of a pentagon. This form was chosen because symbolically it represents the five-pointed star of Bethlehem, the Epiphany star. From a practical point of view, it is an excellent acoustical shape, since none of the five walls of the pentagonal shape are parallel to each other. Parallel walls cause echoes to flutter back and forth, making speech indistinct.

The church seats 800 in pews. These are arranged at reflex angles, a geometry that creates a more relaxed circumstance for the congregation. In keeping with the organic idea that the design of a church should connect to its historical religious context, the sanctuary exemplifies the essential character of the Lutheran faith. Every part relates to and culminates in the focal point of the cross, the symbol representing the direct meeting of God and humanity in Christ.

The architect designed the cross as sculpture that is

Pentagonal light fixtures float overhead and define interior space.

Architecture that touches our creative spirit connects us to divinity.

integral to the architecture. Composed of gold anodized metal, it is a combination of wires and pentagonal shapes that form an ethereal image behind the altar, stretching twenty-six feet across the sanctuary and extending forty feet up to the roof. A skylight below the spire floods the chancel and cross with natural daylight, creating a myriad of tiny points of gold-

en light that shine down to the congregation. The nave is flanked on three sides by balconies for the pipe organ, the choir, and congregation overflow.

Ten pentagonal pendant light fixtures float overhead, defining the interior space. The pentagonal theme is carried through in the design of the pulpit and lectern, the altar, chancel rail, the ends of the

198

pews, even to the shape of the door handles. All were designed by the architect.

The lower level includes a Sunday school, offices, choir practice and social meeting hall. The exterior of the church is finished with marblecrete—white stucco in which are embedded small chips of rose quartz. The interior finish is sand-textured plaster and the floor is carpeted in blue to match the color of the spire and window frames.

Right: *The sanctuary exemplifies the essential character of the Lutheran faith.*

Below: *Symbols of the faith are expressed in every detail.*

DELANO MORTUARY

Delano, California
Date Completed: 1966
William Wesley Peters, Architect

More joyous than funereal, the chapel has a warm and uplifting feeling. It celebrates life.

The idea behind the design of this building is to establish an uplifting atmosphere, one that celebrates the life of a departed soul. The chapel is circular in form, softening the formality of the circumstance, and the triangular-webbed, wood trusses create a forest-like impression. The room is softly lit with indirect sunlight. Illuminated opal glass spheres of varying diameter are woven into the trusses.

The materials are simple. Both exterior and interior walls are concrete block, interwoven so as to create a rich variety of patterns and textures. The star-shaped roof is clad in metal. Its blue-green patina finish relates to the garden court that surrounds the structure. Taliesin designed the interiors, furnishings, and appointments.

More joyous than funereal, the chapel achieves a warm ambience and an uplifting feeling in a quiet and tasteful manner. The spiritual quality of this nondenominational chapel relates to the essence that underlies and unites all faiths and religions.

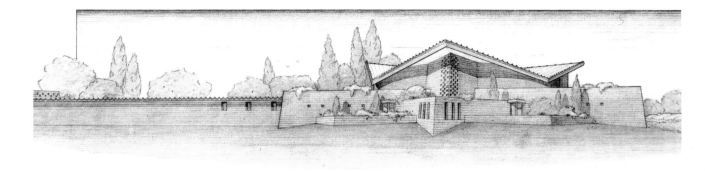

Left: *The spiritual quality of this non-denominational chapel relates to the essence of all faiths.*

Below: *Simple concrete blocks are interwoven to create a rich variety of patterns and textures.*

An ambience that brings people and God closer together.

OUR LADY OF FATIMA CHURCH

Tucson, Arizona
Date Completed: 1976
William Wesley Peters, Architect

Religious buildings include symbols that relate to the ideals and traditions of theology. Some years ago, as the Church began to reconsider their functions, the concept of architectural form underwent a change. The Reverend Peter McGloin of the Tucson Diocese wanted to build a church that inspired worship yet also responded to these changes in both thought and action. His church would not attempt to "contain" God, since God cannot be contained, but it would bring people and God closer together. It would appeal to a younger generation as well as older members.

To reflect the belief that God has trusted humankind to care for the world, Father McGloin believed his church should be beautiful and in harmony with the environment, in this case, the natural Sonoran desert of the Southwest.

Our Lady of Fatima Church consists of a simple and effective space. Its atmosphere is warm and congenial, with a quality that uplifts the spirit. With 400 seats for the congregation, the space is designed to be flexible enough to be used for social events as well as for religious services.

The structural wood members of the roof framing are used as a finished surface. The spire is not the traditional shape but a three-legged abstract design in wrought iron. Taliesin Architects designed all the appointments—the altar, altar cloths, tabernacle, pulpit, and lectern.

The translucent sculpture of "Our Lady of Fatima" by Heloise Christa was designed to be a living, ethereal presence, a being of spirit rather than a realistic representation. Even as spiritual truth is intangible and ineffable, the figure becomes an indefinable vision in the Sanctuary.

Left: *Natural daylight helps to create a feeling of inspiration.*

Below: *The building is in concord with the Sonoran desert.*

RESIDENTIAL

The Myers Residence, Scottsdale, Arizona—the roof fascia breaks up sunlight into ever-changing shadow patterns.

Our goal is to humanize the home, to nurture and inspire the family. Our residential designs create a sense of shelter. Shelter, after all, is the primary function of a house, yet so many house designs do not express this fundamental purpose.

An organic house is a natural house, integral to its site, its environment, and to the life of its inhabitants. We are sensitive to human scale. We design a home not to impress the neighbors but to support the family.

Before we start to design, we visit the site and get to know the client. We want the house to fit the client's needs and to blend with the landscape, since both play an essential role in determining the design. Our houses have both a sense of spaciousness and a

Vaction home for Hamilton McRae's family in Jackson, Wyoming—inspired by the majesty of the Grand Tetons.

Sorenson Residence—the exterior is a natural consequence of what happens inside.

feeling of intimacy and comfort. Balanced daylighting gives warmth to interior spaces, and indirect lighting reduces glare at night. We are sensitive to view opportunities, privacy needs, sun and light controls, and energy demands. Functionality and low maintenance requirements are embodied in the design. Modern technology is incorporated, including electronic systems for lighting, communications, security, audio, video, and management of heating and cooling.

By creating an open flow of space we make a modest-size home seem much larger. A seamless connection between indoor and outdoor space gives a sense of expanse and freedom. We find it a good idea to incorporate some flexibility into a design. If the house is for a couple who are planning to have children, they may need to add bedrooms. The family's need for space will change over the years. After the children have grown up and left, there will be space that may be converted to another use.

People are often astonished that our houses seem so spacious yet are, in reality, usually much smaller than

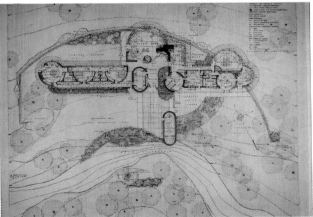

Above: *Sorenson Residence, Black Earth, Wisconsin.*

Left: *Sorenson Residence —a house in love with its site.*

most of the houses being built today. We have liberated the home in many common-sense ways. Designs are created from a point of view of space flow rather than an arrangement of rooms. There is a big difference between moving from space to space and moving from one room into another.

The old formal living room, seldom used, is replaced by an area in which the family feels comfortable. This space in turn flows into other spaces, so that different

207

Klotsche Residence—its graceful curved shapes add to the quality of life lived within.

Model of Klotsche Residence, Santa Fe, New Mexico—interior spaces open onto a garden court.

activities for the family or guests can occur without being confined to boxy rooms. Conversation, entertainment, parties, reading, writing, computers, games, dining, cooking, and so forth are all nicely accommodated. Open areas are contrasted with intimate spaces. A connection to the outdoors adds to the sense of spaciousness. Cabinets are often built in, requiring less room than furniture. There is no wasted space. We often provide a home office and a home theater.

Colors and textures are simple and harmonious. Materials that require minimal maintenance are chosen. Many homes that we designed have been handed down to the next generation.

Just as a person has the aspects of body, mind, and spirit, so should a building. Its body is its form, its shape. Its intelligence is in the way that it functions. Its spirit lies in its humanity, its vitality, its beauty, and its mystery. Like a human being, its exterior countenance is a reflection of its inner quality. Form, intelligence, and spirit must work together in harmony.

A great reward comes to architects when they find that a home they have designed adds an intangible quality to the lives of the family who lives there. When it regenerates those who are tired, sick, or depressed, when it contributes a sense of beauty and joy to their lives and lifts their spirits, it has fulfilled the ideal of organic architecture.

A house is more a home by being a work of art.
                                                                —FLLW

White Residence, Gladwyne, Pennsylvania— form and function joined in spiritual union.

209

BENTON RESIDENCE

Malibu, California
Date Completed: 1985
William Wesley Peters, Architect

Bold geometric roof shapes and texture-patterns define the character of the house.

John Benton grew up as a close friend of the archi-tect's son and developed an appreciation for the phi-losophy of organic architecture. When he and his wife purchased a lot in Malibu, they wanted a house that met the challenge presented by their spectacular property. The far side of their land is a 100-foot-high sheer cliff that drops almost vertically down to the Pacific Ocean.

The design for their home respects and embraces this dramatic site. It is tailor-made, responding to the

Interior space determines what happens on the outside.

The spirit of a home lies in its humanity,
its vitality, its beauty, and its mystery.

The home has a sense of spaciousness and intimacy.

patterns of living and particular needs of the family. Despite the fact that he had no prior experience, John decided to act as his own contractor. This meant that he had to learn as he went along, but it also meant that he could be sure that the construction met high standards of quality. The unforgettable experience of participating in the building of his own home afforded him a sense of pride. He knew where every pipe was buried, every wire concealed. The process took a few years, but the results were admirable.

The house is set just back from the brink of the cliff, far enough to prevent worries about mudslides, but close enough to enjoy the panoramic views. A roof is usually the most significant feature of a residential design, and in this case, the tile roof defines the character of the house. The sculptural tiles were specially made to an inverted V shape. Glazed in a deep-blue color, they connect the house to its ocean setting. The gables of the roof are stepped back in a way that relates the form of the roof to the pattern set by the tiles.

The design of the windows in turn connects to the sloping angles of the roof. Every detail relates to the whole design.

Deep-blue glazed tiles connect to the blue of the Pacific Ocean.

Left: *Quiet elegance—Roman brick walls and copper roofs.*

Below: *The dining terrace extends the interior space into the sunlight.*

KESSLER RESIDENCE

Maplewood, New Jersey
Date Completed: 1968
John Rattenbury, Architect

Dan and Helene Kessler lived with their three children in a small tract house in Maplewood, a village about forty miles from Manhattan. Dan was in the men's clothing business. He had always dreamed of having a beautiful house but did not have the means. When his business started to do well he decided to build his dream house.

When he came to us he had just purchased a large lot in the village of Maplewood. Although this community had only modest-size houses, many of his friends lived there and that is where he wanted to be. His two-acre site was a wooded hillside with fine views of the Manhattan skyline.

The 9,000-square-foot home is constructed with a buff-colored Roman brick with precast concrete cop-

216

Left: *The Entrance Gallery—teak paneling, skylights and tall windows.*

Below: *A space for gracious living. Art objects, collected by the architect came from Japan, China, Italy, Persia, and the U.S.*

ings. The roofing and patterned fascia are patinized copper. The fireplaces are faced with Italian marble, which we selected from the quarry in Italy. The floors are terrazzo, and walls and ceilings are paneled in teak. The workmanship was outstanding and the entire house was built like a Swiss watch.

We custom-designed every aspect of this house, including the light fixtures, the furniture, and cabinetry. Olgivanna Wright was the color consultant. We chose the sculpture, the tableware, and glassware. Many of the art objects we found in Kyoto, Japan. We even selected the leather-bound books for the library. When the clients moved in they brought very little besides their clothes.

The children, Bruce, Rona Sue, and Mark, had bedrooms large enough for an overnight friend to stay. They also had a great playroom on the lower level. For Mark, the youngest, we designed a treehouse, even preparing renderings and construction drawings for his approval. Nestled high in the branches of a giant maple tree, it had steps going up and a pole to slide down. When it was finished, Dan spent the first night with Mark in his organic treehouse.

THE PEARL PALACE AND VILLA MEHRAFARIN

Teheran, Iran
Date Completed: 1973 (P.P.), 1976 (V.M.)
William Wesley Peters, Architect.
John Hill and Cornelia Brierly – Interiors and Landscape design.

The translucent dome spans 120 feet and illuminates everything within.

Princess Shams Pahlavi, the sister of the Shah of Iran, commissioned an Iranian architect, Nezam Amery, to design a small villa for her family—her husband and their two sons. It was to be a prelude to a palace which she planned to build on a large estate at Mehrshahr, near Teheran. Nezam had studied under Frank Lloyd Wright in the fifties. He had designed a handsome villa for the Princess, but when she asked him about designing her palace, he referred her to Wes Peters at Taliesin. This generous act gave Wes the opportunity of his lifetime.

Tales of the Arabian Nights were the stories that Scheherazade told the king every night in order to postpone her death sentence. They had intrigued Wes with their atmosphere of romance and adventure. A student of history and empathetic to the culture of

ancient Persia, Wes dreamed of creating a magic, crystal-domed palace. He took an instant liking to the Princess, a gracious, intelligent, and cultured lady. Her appreciation of beauty and quality stirred his creative abilities. Her most prized jewels, she told him, were her pearls. And so was born in the heart of her creative architect, the Pearl Palace. A translucent dome that spanned 120 feet would enclose garden courts, pools, and sparkling fountains.

The design epitomizes both the culture of historic Persia, where the dome was invented centuries ago, and the achievements of modern technology. A harmonious blend of art and science, the design for the palace pays great respect to both its physical and its cultural environment. The design is infused with the spirit of ancient Persia, but it is a building appropriate to modern times. Another translucent dome encloses gardens, fountains, and the royal reception hall. A gently curving ramp connects to the royal banquet room and family quarters, terminating in a suite for

The Pearl Palace is set on the edge of a lake.

219

the Princess set beneath a marble ziggurat. Intersecting the main dome is another translucent dome that encloses a swimming pool, cascades, and gardens. Below the reception hall is a fully equipped theater for cinema, concerts, and dance performances.

Nezam tells the story of Wes presenting the design to the Princess. As drawing after drawing was laid before her eyes and he explained the scheme, she uttered not a word. When Wes had finished, she stood up and abruptly left the room. A long time elapsed as Wes agonized. Did she not like the design? Perhaps he had offended her. What was the protocol? At last the Princess returned. It was evident that she had been crying. "Forgive me," she said, "it is so incredibly beautiful. I was overwhelmed. All my dreams have come true."

That summer, the Fellowship was staying at Montagnola, Switzerland, occupying the buildings of the American School in Switzerland which was on summer break. John DeKoven Hill worked closely with Wes on the interior design, assisted by Cornelia Brierly, who also designed the landscaping. Between them, these three designed virtually every item in the palace—furniture, carpets, light fixtures, landscaping, uniforms, stationery—nothing was overlooked. Olgivanna

The grand stairway to the reception hall.

Wright oversaw all the fabric and color selections. Everyone at Taliesin pitched in to help with the multitude of details, from mosaic murals to birdcages. The landscaping design included the interior gardens and fountains as well as the entire 100-acre estate. Every item blended with the design theme of the palace. A lovely scale model, complete in every detail, was made in Italy.

The translucent dome was manufactured in the United States by Supersky, flown over and assembled on site. The furnishings were custom-made. Walls were either marble or coated in gold leaf, applied by artisans from the Uffizi Gallery in Florence. Italian craftsmen laid the marble floors, and had to carve seven marble bathtubs in order to get one without a blemish. The Princess could reach her dome-enclosed swimming pool by descending a Lucite stairway, hung from above by slender rods. The gardens contained lush tropical plants, pools, cascades, and fountains, an aviary, and many gold birdcages in the forms of tetrahedrons and octahedrons.

The reception area was encircled by slender gold columns capped with sixty-five, twelve-inch-diameter globes of cut glass, each one an abstract "pearl." Below the reception hall was a movie theater. The royal banquet hall had marble walls inset with semi-circular niches to display jade and ivory figurines and sculptures. Overhead was a five-foot-diameter spherical chandelier of crystal. Made in Vienna, it was assembled on site by women from the factory, crystal by crystal.

The Princess's circular bed was draped with a silk canopy, accented by sparkling crystal pendants. Her bedspread was of gold thread and gold leather appliqué, lit from above by the light of a series of small openings that followed the ascending spiral of a ziggurat.

Wes, Johnny, and Cornelia made many trips to Iran. Tom and Effi Casey spent seven years there, primarily

Villa Mehrafarin—the landscaping is designed as an integral part of the architecture.

Left: *Villa Mehrafin—the summer estate for the Princess Pahlavi's family overlooks the Caspian Sea.*

Below: *Roofs establish the design theme. Individual tiles have the same shape as the roof itself.*

supervising construction of the palace which was built under the direction of contractor/engineer Ara Saginian. In 1972, the Princess and her family moved in. She loved her palace so much that she asked Wes to design a summer villa on a forty-acre estate at Chalus, on the Caspian Sea. Stephen and Frances Nemtin went there to supervise construction of this project, called Mehrafarin Villa. The project was started but never completed, because Iran was upset by a revolution and the Shah was deposed. All the members of the royal family were forced to flee, and the Princess left her beloved palace and moved to Santa Barbara.

For all who were involved in these magical projects, it was a time of exceptional creativity. The buildings are a distinct and unique expression of organic architecture. Like a lovely rose that blooms in a brief moment and then is gone, we are left with a precious memory of ineffable beauty.

The house appears to have grown out of the site—in love with the desert.

MYERS RESIDENCE

Scottsdale, Arizona
Date Completed: 1991
John Rattenbury and Gerry Jones, Architects

The site of the winter home of Charles and Ramona Myers at Desert Highlands is spectacular, strewn with massive sculptured boulders, giant saguaros, Palo Verde trees, and desert wildflowers. Two arroyos or desert washes run across the property, carrying mountain-shed storm water. The Myers wanted their home to complement the natural beauty of their site and provide panoramic views across the valley below. They also wanted their home to have a comfortable, intimate family atmosphere. Congenial hosts, they like to entertain many guests at indoor and outdoor parties.

The 8,000-square-foot house is interwoven with the

The design has a consistent grammar—the shape-relationship between the parts.

Right: *Inspiration for design came from nature's sculpture—giant boulders strewn over the site.*

Below: *The curved forms of walls and domes complement nature.*

granite boulders. Terraced levels and curves wed the plan to the serpentine land contours. During heavy rains, streams of water cross the site. Rather than try to divert the floods, the house consists of three parts interconnected by bridges that span the washes and allow a free flow of storm water. Architectural forms are inspired by nature's desert sculpture—domed roofs, desert colors and textures harmonize with the boulders and patterns of the desert, engaging and blending the house with its environment.

The walls have contrasting textures, some surfaces are sand-textured, and others have fine vertical striations. Constructed of masonry, the walls are faced with exterior insulation and an acrylic coating. A patterned fascia at the roof edge breaks up sunlight to form ever-changing shadow patterns on the walls. The fascia is made of high-density cast-urethane

foam, coated in liquid copper, and patinized to a permanent soft blue-green finish.

Rooms are circular, a shape which captures the sweeping panoramic views across Paradise Valley. Balcony parapets are designed so as to cut off the view of houses in the valley below. Generous terraces extend the indoor space, making a seamless connection with the outdoors. A spiral stair leads to a crow's nest above the living room.

Guests move easily through the spacious, curved contours of the house, finding numerous cozy areas in which to converse. The curved forms are sympathetic to the shape of the human body. Skylights introduce daylight into internal spaces, such as the entry stairwell. The house gives the appearance of having naturally grown out of the desert, a home in love with its environment.

Above left: *Skylights illuminate interior space.*

Above: *The house works well for intimate family life and also accommodates large parties.*

SIMS RESIDENCE

Kamuela, Hawaii
Date Completed: 1995
John Rattenbury, Architect
Kay Rattenbury, Interior Designer

One day we received an unusual phone call: "My name is Sandy Sims," said the caller, "and I have this idea of building a collection of Frank Lloyd Wright-designed houses in Hawaii. They would be original designs that were never built. By creating a 'village' we would have something unique in the world, real estate that was a work of art. Can I come over and discuss this with you?" Sandy came to Taliesin West and we showed him the treasures in our archives. This made him even more enthusiastic about his idea.

Sandy talked to many investors and raised some interest. Realizing that his credibility would go up if one house were built, he purchased land on the high

At night the warmth and beauty of the interior is revealed to outside view.

228

The solar hemicycle house embraces the sun and ocean views.

Right: *The lower level is a free-flowing open space that includes several alcoves.*

Below: *The kitchen works well for one or for many cooks. Friends love to sit and chat.*

slopes above the Mauna Kea Hotel and there built an unexecuted design by Frank Lloyd Wright.

The 3,700-square-foot solar hemicycle house fits the site perfectly. It faces a broad view of the Kohala coastline below, while its uphill side is bermed to protect it from the strong trade winds. The walls are cement blocks, made from buff-colored coral found in the Hawaiian reefs. The sculptured fascia has a blue-green copper patina. People have remarked that the home not only blends with its site, but even seems to have some Polynesian flavor. This is no doubt due to the soaring curves of the roof.

The workmanship is excellent. When craftsmen have the opportunity to work on a beautiful design, it seems to bring out the best in them. The chairs and lamps are original Wright designs. In 1996, the house received the Hawaiian Cement Achievement Award for the best new residence in Hawaii.

Sandy's wife, Suzanne, uses the house to conduct week-long retreats, bringing artists, philosophers, and creative minds together for a remarkable learning experience. Sandy is still pursuing his idea to build a collection of unexecuted Wright designs.

From time to time, they allow people to rent their house for a few days or weeks. They realize that very few people have the chance to ever stay in a Frank Lloyd Wright home. Those who own a Wright home have a remarkable day-to-day experience, but it is one that does not transfer to other people. Guests who have stayed at the Sims house have expressed profound appreciation for the experience.

The idea of three-dimensional space-flow offers many exciting possibilities.

THEILEN RESIDENCE

Dallas, Texas
Date Complete: 1993
John Rattenbury, Architect.
Kay Rattenbury, Interior Designer

The house is designed to nurture the family.

Dr. George Theilen and his wife, Jan, owned a choice lot on a cul-de-sac. Located in a quiet neighborhood of suburban Dallas, the site has some wonderful old oak trees. The land slopes gently down to a creek.

George is an obstetrician, and Jan studied home eco-nomics in college. They had given some thought as to how they wanted their house planned. "We have four sons," they said, "but only give us three children's bed-rooms. The younger two can bunk together. By the time they need their own bedrooms, our oldest son will be in college, and his room will be free. Give them a playroom where they can watch TV and use a computer. They need a way to get out to the pool, and they should have a poolhouse, which their friends can also use. We want the children to enjoy the house while they grow up, but one day they will leave, so concentrate on making the house comfortable for us. We want a separate master bedroom. We don't need a garage; a carport is fine."

Tall, mitered glass windows connect the house to the creek.

Right: *All the details sing together in harmony.*

Below: *A space that is both informally comfortable and aesthetically pleasing*

The Theilens were not interested in showing off to their neighbors, so the house is unpretentious from the street. The walls are Indiana limestone, laid up with some of the horizontal stones projecting out from the face of the wall. The roof fascia has a blue-green patinized copper and the window frames match this color.

The living room is the center of family life, and features a broad stone fireplace. A tall, mitered glass window, with a view down to the creek, makes a seamless connection to the outdoors. Clerestory windows provide a nice balance of natural daylight. Space flows from one room to another and doors are limited to bedrooms and bathrooms.

We designed all the furniture and the built-in cabinets. The wood is red oak with a natural finish. We custom designed the carpet, which was woven in India. The house fits the family and it fits the site, with the quality of true simplicity. Its elegance is informal and understated.

FOCUS HOUSE AT TALIESIN GATES

Scottsdale, Arizona
Date Completed: 1987
William Wesley Peters, Architect.
Cornelia Brierly, Interior Designer

An opportunity to experiment with a new way to build houses came to us when we decided to con-struct a 4,300-square-foot model spec house using our own resources. Set on a rise in the desert below Taliesin West, with the MacDowell Mountains as a backdrop, the house faces south and looks across Paradise Valley.

The house is a passive-solar design, framed with light steel studs and joists. Walls are composed of expanded polystyrene, coated with fiberglass-reinforced plaster. The finish is an acrylic-cement textured coating, col-ored to blend with the Sonoran desert. The walls have a sawtooth or corrugated configuration. Inspired by the

Vertical striations in the walls create a slow dance of shadow patterns.

Right: *The fireplace
echoes the sculptural forms
of the house.*

Below: *The house is
attuned to the site in form,
color and texture—an
abstraction of the desert.*

ribs of the Saguaro cactus, the pleated folds give
strength to the walls and, at the same time, create ever-
changing patterns of light and shadow.

The focal point of the living room is a sculptured
fireplace, composed of the same vertical corrugations
as the walls. The interior space connects seamlessly to
the view terrace. Shade for the terrace and glass wall
is provided by metal louvers. Motor-operated, they
automatically close to shade the windows, then open
to let in more light as the angle of the sun changes.

There are four bedrooms, each one having access to
the terrace and swimming pool. The master bedroom has
an enormous walk-in closet and its own outdoor spa.

Nine months of the year, the climate in Scottsdale
allows for outdoor living, so the 2,500–square-foot
roof terrace is a useful luxury. A dumbwaiter services
a pantry and wet bar. The roof deck provides a perfect place to relax and watch as the Arizona sun sets
behind Camelback Mountain and the city lights start
to twinkle. A great house for entertaining, its human
scale makes it comfortable for family life.

The ceiling is a mosaic of plywood panels.

Living space of Sunsprite opens to terraces on either side—sunlight embraced but controlled.

SUNSPRITE AND SUNSTREAM

Palm Desert, California
Date Completed: 1988
John Rattenbury, Architect

Designing a model or spec house is a challenge because the family who will live there can provide no input. Their surrogate during the design phase is partly the developer, partly the architect. This provides a degree of design freedom, but also brings the responsibility of making predictions on what will sell. A good developer doesn't want the architect to just copy the style currently in vogue, but gives the architect an opportunity to redefine the American home.

When the Marriott Corporation built the Desert Springs Resort, they ended up with extra land and decided to create a residential subdivision with thirty-four lots. We were asked to design the first two homes

Simplicity in the plan comes from having no corridors and few doors.

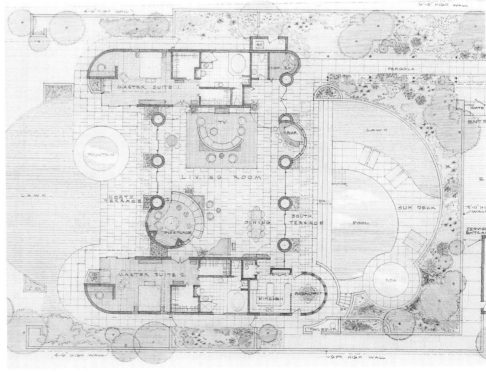

Above: *Sunsprite—one space flows into another, interchanging, intermixing.*

Right: *The living area is both spacious and cozy.*

as pacesetters. Potential buyers were identified as corporate executives attuned to an active social entertainment life-style.

Sunsprite is a house that takes full advantage of the desert climate. Rather than designing a 3,600-square-foot building on a half-acre lot (21,000 square feet), the entire lot became the plan of the house. Exterior and interior spaces are interwoven. The property fronts a golf course and this also becomes part of the space experience, visually expanding the "design envelope." The arrival experience starts at a gate to the covered walk, or pergola. Walking through the lush garden up to the front door, one has, in effect, already "entered" the house.

The main living area has 1,500 square feet of space but seems even larger since it opens on one side to a swimming pool, spa, and garden, and on the other to a fountain and the golf course. The space is naturally divided into areas, fireplace and sunken conversation area, dining, entertainment, sit-down bar. Flanking

Sunstream—wall surfaces resonate with the textures of the desert.

241

Above: *From the street, Sunstream is quiet and unassuming.*

Right: *The plan spreads the house out into the garden and brings the garden into the house.*

this space are two luxurious master suites. Guests move freely onto the terraces, shaded by deep roof overhangs.

The second house, Sunstream, takes the open space plan a step further. The house is decentralized, with four bedrooms placed in a detached wing, connected by a covered walkway. The wedge-shaped lot is only forty-one feet wide at the golf course, yet due to the configuration of the house, every room has a view of the fairway. The house is wrapped around a swimming pool, spa, and garden court. Sunstream, like its sister Sunsprite, has privacy from its neighbors and is unpresuming from the street. The quality of both is warm and optimistic, able to handle many guests at a party, yet cozy and comfortable for a small family.

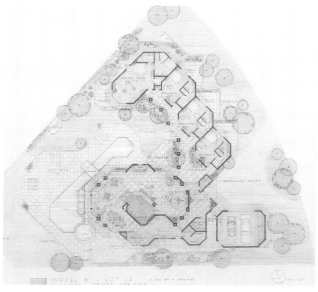

The living area is spacious, with cozy areas for the family.

The sweeping branches of the giant sequoia inspired the design.

WINDINTIDE

Edmunds, Washington
Date Completed: 1994
Stephen Nemtin, Architect

The home of Richard and Erin Weight is a grace to the landscape, and the natural beauty of the site permeates the house. Perched on a bluff thick with ever-greens, it overlooks the blue waters of Puget Sound.

The sweeping branches of a giant sequoia that hover over the house gave inspiration to the design. The poetry of their form is captured in the curved fins that support the roof. The Sound becomes a presence in the home and is intimately connected to it by a cantilevered balcony that soars over a natural ravine. This balcony wraps both wings of the house and extends the interior space outdoors. Despite the dynamic aspect of the cantilever, the house maintains

Puget Sound becomes a presence inside the home.

245

a sense of serenity and quiet repose.

While the home provides a snug shelter from the elements, through the imaginative use of glass, nature is invited inside. From every interior space one has glimpses of sky, forest, and water, with each view framed differently. A continuous skylight brings in daylight.

Careful siting allowed the house to be built without the need to cut down trees. Cedar siding blends harmoniously with the bark of the evergreens. Natural cross ventilation obviates the need for air conditioning, and radiant heating in the floor makes the home comfortable in winter. All the floors are Brazilian cherry. The warmth of this rich wood further unifies interior space.

LYKES/MELTON RESIDENCE

Phoenix, Arizona
Date Complete: 1995
John Rattenbury, Architect

At a time when there were only dirt roads to Taliesin West, Norman and Aimee Lykes and their four children lived in a ranch house nearby. They asked Frank Lloyd Wright to design a new home on a one-acre lot in Saguaro Canyon. The steeply sloping land had a mountain backdrop and spectacular views.

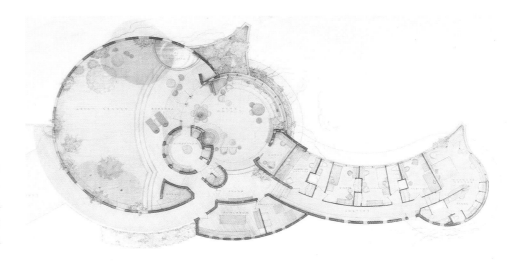

Above: *The shape of the plan follows the natural contours of the land.*

Left: *Nestled in the rocks, the house adds to the natural beauty of the site.*

After studying the topographic map, Wright set it aside for a while and worked on other projects. He always allowed an idea to germinate before committing it to paper. The next morning he quickly sketched a plan right on the map. "This is where the house belongs," he said, pointing to a small flat area halfway up the steeply sloped property. There was a beautiful rock outcropping nearby which he wanted to save.

With the panoramic view in mind, and considering the shape of the natural plateau, he drew two overlapping circles. As he drew, he explained his sketch. "Here is the living room with a view over the valley. The bedrooms will wrap the hillside, on the far side of the house. Here is the carport, the entrance, and then a step down to the living room with a grand view over Phoenix. Below the windows is a built-in seat, big enough for all the children. The fireplace is the heart of the house, its anchor. They need an outdoor space, but must have privacy from their neighbors, so we will give them a garden court with a wall around it."

After a while, Wright got up from his desk and walked out of the studio. He never returned. The next day he was in the hospital with an intestinal problem, and a few days later, on April 9, 1959, he died. In two months he would have been ninty-two. He had many projects underway but this was the last house that he designed. We completed the drawings and the house was built. The Lykes family loved their home and lived there for many years.

The broad roof-overhangs express both a sense of shelter and a kinship to the ground, and the horizontal lines of the house create a sense of repose. A continuous clerestory window around the circular living

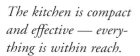

The kitchen is compact and effective — everything is within reach.

248

The living room—panoramic views over the city and an enclosed garden court to the north.

room provides a balance of soft natural light. Indoor space connects to outdoor space in a seamless flow and the house expresses a sense of freedom. Its round shapes are more inviting and comfortable to live in than straight lines and square corners.

In 1993 Linda Melton purchased the house. She needed to make the interior space more appropriate to her needs but was determined to keep the integrity of the design intact, so no changes were made to the exterior. No cracks had appeared in the masonry in thirty years so the walls and roof framing were left untouched. Some modifications were made inside the bedroom wing—adding the space of another bedroom enlarged the master bedroom. Two children's bedrooms were combined to make a guestroom. The workshop became a home theater.

New air-conditioning and electrical systems were installed, along with new lighting and plumbing fixtures. The mahogany woodwork was refinished, a slate floor was added.

The Lykes summer cottage was designed for a steep and heavily wooded site near the little village of Tuxedo in North Carolina. A mountain stream carries rushing water downhill and rhododendron bushes grow in profusion. In order not to destroy but enjoy this beauty, the cottage is designed as a bridge that spans the stream. Two steel girders salvaged from an old highway bridge provide structural support. To conserve space, there are eight bunk beds for children that fold into the wall like Pullman berths.

The office is a crow's nest with views all around.

A HOUSE FOR LIFE

Gold Mountain, California
Date Completed: 1997
John Rattenbury, Architect

The *Life Magazine* Dream House of 1997 was our opportunity to design a home for a family of moderate means and make the plans available to the public at an affordable cost. Steve Petranek, the editor, wanted to raise the standard of house design in America. He had the idea of asking architects to design a dream house. *Life* would publish the design and sell the plans.

The 2,100-square-foot home is designed with adaptable space that responds to the needs of an American family today. Its many variations and options work for all types of families: unmarried, married with or with-

Above: *The design serves the needs of a young couple, a growing family, or a couple in retirement.*

Right: *America's dream is a moderate-cost, high-quality home.*

out children, mixed generations, and retired people. It meets the needs of a family as it moves through the different stages of life. It can start with two bedrooms and expand as needed to three or four.

To adapt to different parts of the country, various climates, and site possibilities, there is a choice of several different roof configurations. For a suburban lot, there is privacy from the street and neighbors. Broad overhangs create a sense of shelter and extend indoor space outwards. Those who have built the house are surprised that it is so spacious. Simple, sensible, natural, in human scale, with a timeless quality, the house is designed to nurture a family for life.

For the *Life* Dream House series, the magazine usually published an architect's design drawings. We wanted to make the dream a reality and build it before

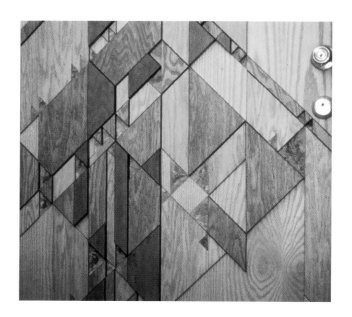

The 1997 Life *Dream House has many variations of floor plans and roof types.*

it was published. We had master planned a residential community called Gold Mountain, about forty miles north of Lake Tahoe. They wanted a model house, so we started to build the *Life* Dream House. We had only a few months to do this, and winters in the Sierra Nevada Mountains are severe. The deadline for the photoshoot was in February. When the photographer arrived, the house was not yet finished. The masons were starting to build the fireplace but the finish floor had not been laid, the windows were not completed, cabinetwork not installed. Working night and day, the building team finished it in four days. The photos of the furnished interior that appeared in the magazine are evidence of their outstanding effort.

Over 600 sets of plans have been sold in the United States. People who have built it comment on how well it works. We are grateful for the opportunity to make a contribution to moderate-cost housing in America.

Above: *The Master Suite, separated from the children's wing, has its own covered porch.*

Left: *The heart of the house is the fireplace and entertainment center.*

PRODUCTION HOUSING

The house of moderate cost is not only America's major architectural problem but also the problem most difficult for her architects.

—FLWR

No house is just like another — each has its own individuality.

Most families prefer to live in a single-family home, but many people cannot afford custom-designed, site-built houses. Production housing is a way to build houses more economically, either in the factory or in the field. In the factory, manufacturing and prefabrication methods utilize the assembly line and controlled environment. In the field, site-built production houses employ repetition of design and construction to achieve economy.

As a result of the enormous demand for housing, the country has been flooded with tract housing and mobile home parks, many of which contribute to urban blight. In an effort to improve the quality of affordable housing, the Wisconsin Department of National Resources commissioned us to conduct a

Small homes based on the open-space concept seem much larger.

255

study. Our report noted the shortcomings of manufactured home designs and proposed some solutions
for improvement. This led the National Homes
Corporation, the largest manufacturer of mobile and
modular houses in the country, to ask us to design
their new line of production housing.

Through simple modifications, such as changing the
end of a mobile home to eliminate its box shape,
removing unnecessary trim, and relating the unit to
the ground, we made some inexpensive but significant
improvements. It was the first time that the mobile
home industry had seen designs that looked like permanent homes instead of cheap metal boxes. Mobile
homes are usually stacked in rows and placed in a park
that looks more like a parking lot.

Although cheap to buy, mobile homes are not a
good investment. They have a much shorter life than
site-built houses and they depreciate rather than

appreciate in value. They add little to the quality of life of their occupants. And while it is normally easier to maintain higher standards of quality in products built in the factory than in the field, unfortunately this is not the case with mobile homes. The market is highly competitive and profit margins are tight. The nature of the factory line discourages innovations because they disrupt production flow. However, in our work with National Homes, we did institute some good ideas and enhancements, even if we couldn't reinvent the process.

Our designs extended into the field of modular houses—factory-made houses shipped to the site as three-dimensional units. We also designed prefabricated houses made from panelized walls and roofs. Later we designed a mobile home for an Arizona Company, International Homes Corporation, which was run by Joni Hegel. We laid out her mobile home park, Paradise

Left: *Production housing takes advantage of factory techniques to reduce costs.*

Below: *A mobile home design for the National Homes Corp.—simple ways to make them better.*

257

Peak West, using covered terraces to extend the rooflines, harmonious colors, and landscaping to create an attractive community.

In addition to factory-built units, production housing includes houses that are repetitively produced in the field. Russ Riggs, a local homebuilder, approached us to design a residential community called Mountain View Estates. It contained fifty-six single-story houses on forty acres. Russ wanted to get away from the tract house syndrome, where every house looks like a copy of the one next door. At the same time, he needed economical designs because the market is so competitive.

Our solution was to design six floor plans for customers to choose from, and then create a different elevation and roof design for each one of the fifty-six houses. We also customized a plan if the customer wished. They could choose from a palette of desert colors. and the entire community was generously landscaped with trees and shrubs. The result was a community that has a sense of place, harmony, and

unity, and at the same time, variety, because no two houses were exactly alike.

The project was a big success, so Russ came to us with another walled-community project, Mountain View East, fifty-one houses on thirty acres. With the experience of Mountain View Estates under our belts, we simplified the concept, designing five floor plans. Each plan had options of different roof designs. Four of the plans were single-story and one was two-story. By flipping plans and intermixing elevations and desert colors, we achieved variety. Each house looks different from its neighbor.

For another client, we designed an affordable house made with lightweight concrete. The concrete was poured in place on the site and the forms were reused for the next house.

The ideas that we developed for production housing did create some small improvements in the industry. But while the need is essential and the tools are at hand, progress in the production housing industry barely creeps ahead.

Everybody has an enclosed private pool, shaded terrace and garden.

MASTER PLANNING

Make no little plans; they have no magic to stir man's blood.
—Daniel H. Burnham

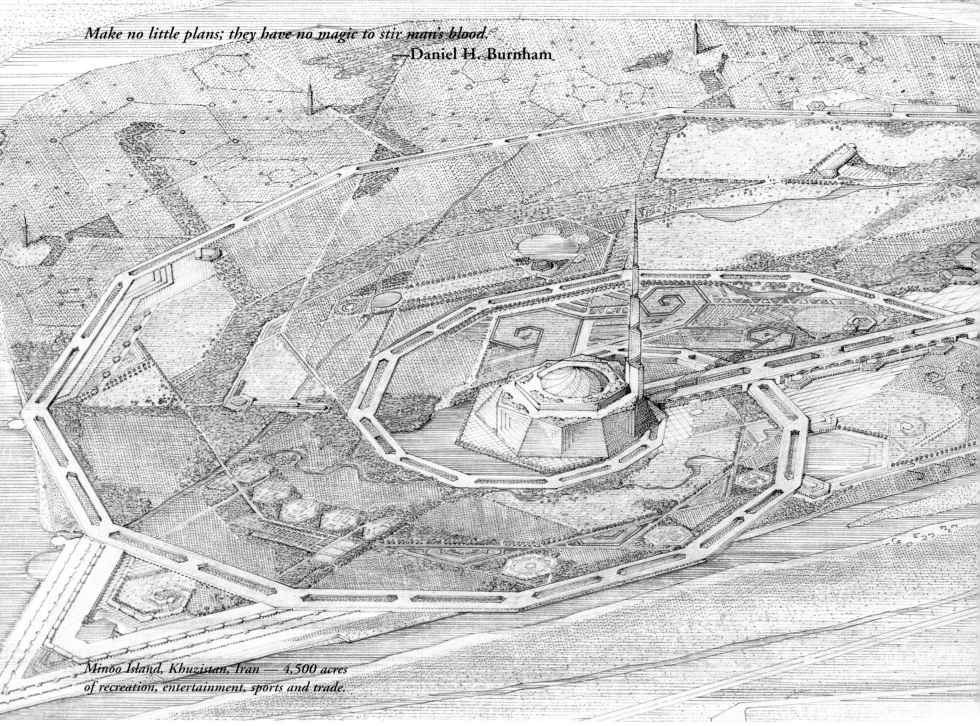

Minoo Island, Khuzistan, Iran — 4,500 acres of recreation, entertainment, sports and trade.

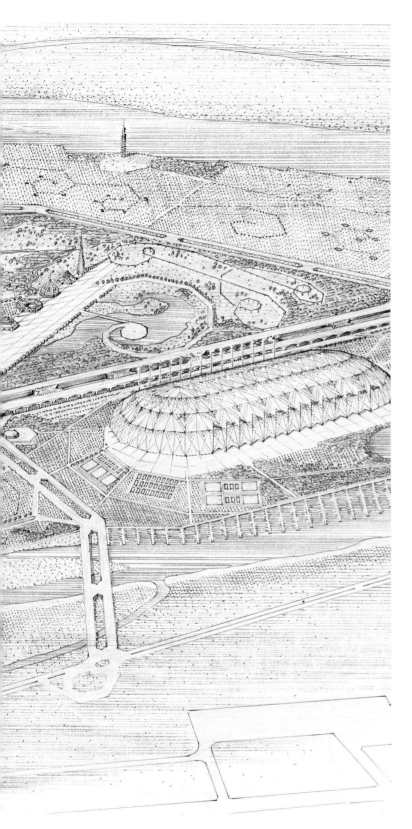

The projects that we have master planned range from a few acres up to 100,000 acres. They include residential and mixed-use developments, urban redevelopment, resorts, civic centers, college campuses, office and industrial parks, health care, golf communities, zoos, and interstate highways. In these projects we have pioneered ways to develop the land without destroying the landscape.

Humankind's greatest physical asset is the earth. Once we have destroyed a piece of the land, it may take a hundred years or more to regenerate. In some

Kohler Village in Wisconsin, a 2,000-acre, mixed-use master plan.

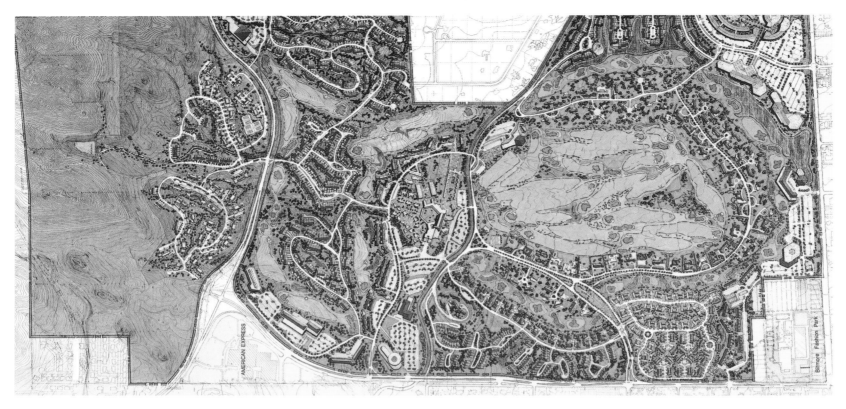

Arizona Biltmore Estates, Phoenix, Arizona—a 1,045-acre, mixed-use master plan.

cases, it is lost forever. Every year, enormous areas of forest and jungle are devastated. We are slowly realizing the global effects of this irresponsibility.

There are many ways that we harm our planet. Expedient developments that are poorly planned and disrespectful of land formations, vegetation, and natural features. Buildings that are not energy conservative. Poor quality in design and construction. Air pollution, contamination of our oceans, lakes, and rivers. Toxic waste, garbage dumps. Noise pollution. Poles, wires, and billboards. Land laid waste by war, land mines, Agent Orange, atomic waste. These acts could all be avoided.

We are at last acknowledging our role as stewards of our planet and our responsibility to think beyond our own lifetimes. We can be grateful to the courageous pioneers of our country who left us a legacy of freedom and a land of opportunity, but what heritage will we leave to future generations? Surely something more than a planet that we have abused in order to get as

much for ourselves as fast as possible.

Our own land planning efforts strike a balance between the economic goals of the developer and the environmental concerns of jurisdictional agencies. We have proved that planning in harmony with the landscape dramatically increases property values. We have been called Land Lovers, and plead guilty to the allegation. Nevertheless, the projects that we plan make good profits for investors and raise the standard for what constitutes excellence.

Planning is a complex team effort, requiring the coordinated participation of many consultants and specialists. These may include surveyors, civil engineers, and environmental, legal, political, social, geological, hydrological, transportation, parking, and public relations consultants, and many others. In our experience, it is far easier to unite the efforts of this multidisciplinary team when the goal is to plan a project that seeks innovative ways to preserve and harmonize with nature. Obtaining approvals from governmental agencies is also easier, since their goal is usually the same.

Establishing real human and spiritual values and then applying thoughtful and sensitive planning are the first steps towards ensuring a better future.

Many of us deplore the lack of beauty and harmony in our built environment, but what can we do? When you look at a city, a community, or a suburb, what would you choose to do, if you had a magic wand? With this wand, in one magic stroke, you could change just one thing, but it would affect all buildings. How could you best harmonize them with their environment? Well, consider color control. Imagine all structures in colors sympathetic with the natural environment (this would still allow hundreds of color tones). Many planned communities are recognizing the importance of color, and although architectural forms are widely varied (as they should be), a universal palette of earth tone colors brings a sense of concord to the whole, at no additional expense.

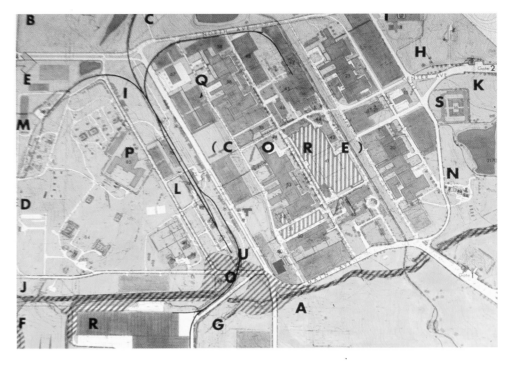

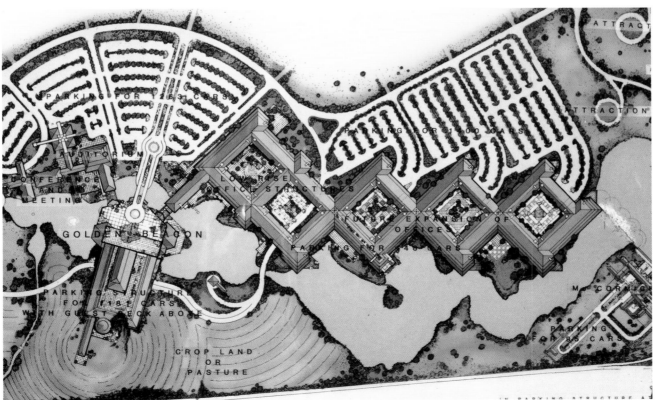

Above: *The Denver Federal Center—coordinating 27 government agencies on 670 acres.*

Left: *Domino World Farms in Alma, Michigan—a plan for 1.4 million square feet of offices.*

263

Taliesin and International Engineering designed 20 award-winning bridges on I-70.

VAIL PASS

Colorado
Date completed: 1971
Charles Montooth, Architect

In the late sixties, as our nation started to become aware of the fragility of nature and realize its responsibility for protection of the natural environment, an interstate highway was planned in Colorado. Between Denver and Vail, the proposed route for I-70 passes through one of most beautiful scenic areas in the Rocky Mountains. A fourteen-mile stretch, this four-lane highway runs through a wilderness area of rugged mountains, pristine forests, and over cascading rivers. Because of our long history of designing projects that are harmonious with nature, we were chosen as design consultants in the team of engineers, biologists, geologists, and ecologists that would plan this major transportation corridor. The team was commissioned to prepare a comprehensive study of the impact that the highway would have on the area—ecology, scenic values, wildlife, hiking and skiing trails, and air quality.

The rugged terrain would require seventeen highway bridges, most of them long span, as well as many large-scale retaining walls. Our task was to guide the

Colors, forms, and textures were carefully chosen to blend with the terrain.

design of these structures so that they would blend with the environment. The goal was to feature the works of nature, not the works of people.

For countless hours the team hiked over the route, studying the mountain slopes, valleys, meadows, watercourses, and small communities along the route. In the engineering design of the bridges and the structures to retain earth, forms and shapes were kept as simple as possible. Colors and textures were selected to be sympathetic with the surrounding landscape. The watchword was as little intrusion on nature as possible. The summit shelter is constructed of stone masonry and utilizes a solar collector for heating in wintertime.

The project received numerous awards, but the greatest compliments are silent ones. They come from the thousands of people who drive the highway every day and enjoy the unspoiled beauty of nature. The evidence of human intrusion has virtually vanished.

Right: *The innovative designs of retaining walls provides areas for plants to grow.*

Below: *The highway follows the natural curves of the land, always responsive to nature.*

DESERT HIGHLANDS

Scottsdale, Arizona
Date completed: 1980
John Rattenbury, Planner

In 1980, a friend, Hamilton McRae, introduced us to Lyle Anderson. Lyle had just purchased 826 acres of land in rural Maricopa County. Upgrading to commercial zoning would increase the value of the land, so he decided to include a hotel in the master plan. At first we were only involved in the hotel design, but after we had worked with Lyle for a while he gave us the task of master planning the property.

From the start, he agreed that we should seek ways to build in harmony with the land. This gave us the opportunity to pioneer some ideas in sensitive land planning. In the midst of the entitlement process with the county, the city of Scottsdale annexed the area. We had to resubmit for master plan approval, but the city endorsed our plan because they appreciated its goal of preserving the environment. The idea for a hotel was replaced with a championship golf course designed by Jack Nicklaus.

The natural features of the site—the topography, views, solar orientation, land forms, vegetation, and drainage areas, all informed us how to best plan the property. In an inspired moment, Lyle tied lot sales to a membership in the golf club. Sales boomed, and his prediction of the viability of a low-density residential/golf community was confirmed.

Our major contribution to the planning was to

Residences and golf harmoniously blend with the natural desert.

work out innovative ways to build without destroying the desert. At the time, most developers were scalping the land and creating huge flat pads on which to build. They saw trees and rocks as obstructions to construction. At Desert Highlands, the roads were carefully constructed so as to have minimal impact on the landscape. Utilities were all placed underground. Great care was taken to restore any damaged desert to a natural condition. Special techniques were developed for transplanting desert vegetation.

The idea of establishing a "building envelope" on every lot is a way to preserve the fragile desert. Each lot that is sold has a designated area within which the

Right: *Jack Nicklaus and team planning the golf course to blend with nature.*

Below: *Mass and height are limited, only desert colors and textures are allowed.*

Left: *Design guidelines and reviews ensure harmony with the environment.*

Below: *Pioneering the concept of the "building envelope" as the way to preserve nature.*

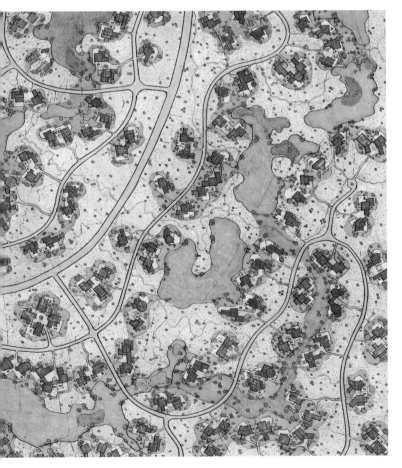

house can be built. The land outside this envelope is protected during construction by a chain link fence.

The design of every residence is submitted to a review committee for approval, and stringent design guidelines ensure that every building is harmonious in mass, color, and texture with the environment. Reflective surfaces, such as glass, are shaded from the sun.

The green fairways of a golf course are a good way to make the arid desert less hostile, but unless care is taken, the irrigated areas change forever the natural vegetation of the desert. This is resolved by creating a buffer zone that keeps water strictly confined to the grass areas of the golf course. Landscaping at each residence is restricted to plant species compatible with the desert.

Desert Highlands is one of our most successful master plans. It set the standard for how to build in harmony with the desert, and many communities have adopted similar methods of planning and development. Taking such care to preserve the landscape does increase development costs, compared to bulldozing everything flat, but it is a wise investment. The value of the land increases dramatically because people are willing to pay much more to live in a community where they can forever enjoy the beauty of nature.

269

DESERT MOUNTAIN

Scottsdale, Arizona
Date completed: 1984
John Rattenbury, Planner

Desert Mountain is an 8,500-acre master plan for land that has almost no flat areas.

Four years after we started planning Desert Highlands, Lyle Anderson acquired control of a much larger piece of property, 8,100 acres. Preparing the conceptual plan for this project was a big task. What a responsibility—to plan such an incredibly beautiful piece of land and develop it in a way that would not mar its natural beauty.

Although the planning of Desert Highland had been done without the aid of computers, on Desert Mountain we were able to use advanced technology. Aerial mapping helped us identify the topography of the terrain, which covered more than twelve square

miles. In order to identify and understand its complex natural features, we walked almost every bit of the land. Many hiking boots were worn out during this process.

The north end of the property includes some spectacular mountains. It abuts the Tonto National Forest, the fourth largest national forest in the United States. None of the land at Desert Mountain is flat, everything is three-dimensional. The landforms are undulated, with multiple ridges and valleys. From the south end of the property, the land rises 2,300 feet to the north end. The desert vegetation is lush, with thousands of giant saguaros, palo verde trees, rock formations, boulders, and deep arroyos. We filled a large room with topographic maps, slope analyses, studies of hydrology, geology, vegetation, and views. Only after exhaustive studies to fully understand what we were dealing with did we let our imagination loose.

Our philosophy was to never build on ridgelines or mountain slopes, and to preserve as much of the landscape as possible. People who come to Desert Mountain for the first time are amazed that the houses and buildings blend into the desert so effectively.

The project was planned to have thirty separate gated villages. Natural features, arroyos, and ridges that run down from the mountain slopes, often determine the size and shape of each village. This decentralization gives the whole community a more human scale and also allows the project to be sensibly phased. At least forty percent of the land in each village is open space, and 2,600 acres are dedicated to a natural mountain preserve.

A multitude of decisions must be made on a project of this scale—hasty developments often get into trouble. It takes a sizeable investment to bring the project to a point where lots can be sold. Although all projects are driven to a large extent by the vagaries of the market, those of high quality and integrity have a better chance of riding the economic waves. This requires courage, patience, and staying power. Desert Mountain has an unwavering commitment—to protect and preserve the sensitive desert environment and provide world-class

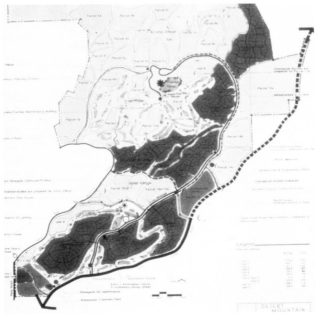

Above: *The planners made an exhaustive study of the land. They walked over it for days, photographed and mapped it until they understood it.*

Left: *There are nine villages and five golf courses.*

land planning. Everything is carefully considered—golf course design and construction, residences, amenities—every element integral to the success of a private residential community. All are designed and constructed in harmony with the natural environment.

One of the first things constructed was a scenic drive through the property. A drive through beautiful terrain, virtually undisturbed by development, is the best of all sales agents. During the process of installing this road and constructing the first golf course, over one hundred thousand native trees and shrubs were carefully dug up and stored at an on-site nursery. Later they were replanted, as part of the pro-

Left: *The Ingersoll Residence is designed to blend with a natural rock outcropping.*

Below: *The house over-looks the golf course.*

gram to revegetate every piece of the land that was disturbed during development.

Land sales at Desert Mountain have remained consistent throughout the past fifteen years. There are now five Jack Nicklaus golf courses: Renegade, Cochise, Geronimo, Apache, and Chiricahua. There are four golf clubhouses and a swim, fitness, and tennis center. Design and development guidelines ensure that all homes blend with the desert landscape. Everything at Desert Mountain is done thoughtfully, with total respect for the fragile beauty of the land. The developer is pleased with its economic success and the homeowners have good reason to be so proud of their community.

THE PHOENIX ZOO

Phoenix, Arizona
Date completed: 1987
John Rattenbury, Planner

Some years ago, zoos around the world began to implement a major change. Instead of displaying animals in cages for people to stare at, they became dedicated to the preservation, breeding, care, and protection of animals. It has become as important to protect animals from people as people from animals. The Phoenix Zoo, now the most extensive private zoo in the United States, along with other zoos in the country, is saving several species from extinction.

As closely as possible, animals are given a home that simulates their native habitat. The exhibits are mostly multispecies, since many different species are usually found in the same habitat. Bars and cages are used as little as possible, replaced by large landscaped areas separated from people by dry or wet moats. Plant life is nurtured along with animal life, and whenever possible the trees and shrubs are native to each habitat.

The Phoenix Zoo pioneered this step forward in zoology, but although they were taking steps to make the change, they lacked a comprehensive long-range plan. Working closely with the Dr. Savoy, the director, Ralph Jones, Curator of Design, and the Arizona Zoological Society, we prepared a master plan.

The African Veldt at the Phoenix Zoo—visitors discover animals as they are in nature.

Six different habitats are included in the 126-acre park—Desert, Savanna, Woodland, Tropical Forest, Aquatic, and Riparian. There is an abundance of water available, thanks to the Arizona Canal system which passes through the property. Attendance at the zoo increased rapidly, and crowd handling was part of our study. Pedestrian trails and a sixty-five-seat zoo train link the different habitats. There is also a delightful children's zoo.

We designed several of the animal exhibits as well as an education complex. One of our goals was to create for the visitors a sense of discovery, to echo the delight of finding animals in the wild. As people are entertained, they are also educated about animals, ecosystems, and how people relate to nature. The Phoenix Zoo is doing its part for the betterment of our planet's future.

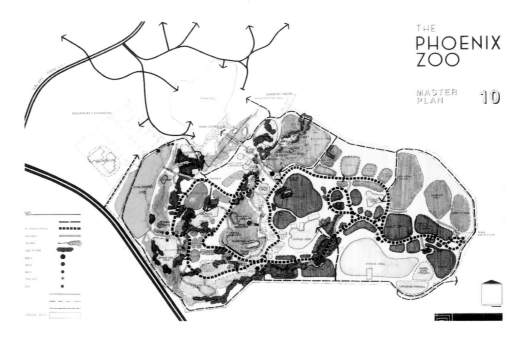

THE
PHOENIX
ZOO

MASTER
PLAN 10

Above: *Habitats include Desert, Savannah, Woodland, Tropical, Aquatic, Riparian.*

Left: *Animals are not exhibited, but observed in their natural habitat.*

GOLD MOUNTAIN

Plumas County, California
Date completed: 2000
Arnold Roy, Architect

Dariel and Peggy Garner are a courageous couple, imaginative, entrepreneurial, and hard working. They started an agricultural business in Baja Mexico, raising specialty vegetables, a subject they knew little about at the time but soon turned into a successful venture. After selling it at a profit, they decided to build an ocean-view home in southern Oregon. Unable to acquire the lot they wanted, they looked for another one. To find the perfect place for their house became a quest that took them all over the western United States and eventually to Australia and New Zealand. They knew they wanted a home designed by Taliesin Architects, but couldn't acquire the right property, although they made offers on twenty-five different lots.

The model shows how the design fits the terrain and is at home in the pine forest.

Far left: *The golf course is carefully woven into the forest.*

Above: *The Nakoma
Country Club was
designed 85 years ago.*

Right: *1,200 acres of private forest in the Sierra
Nevada mountains.*

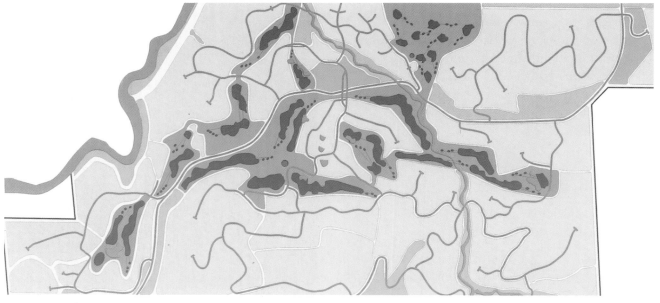

Finally they found the right one—a beautiful piece of land near Graeagle in the Sierra Nevada mountains of California, forty miles north of Lake Tahoe. It was more than a lot. It was a pristine forest area next to the Feather River—over 1,200 acres.

They asked us to help create a sensitive development plan for this spectacular property. We commenced the process by holding a visioning session on site, inviting questions and comments from the community. After specific goals were defined in a mission statement, we prepared a master plan concept for homes and a golf course, carefully laid out so as to preserve the natural beauty of the land. There are 427 spectacular lots ranging from excellent to incredible. To the west is Mount Eureka, the mountain named after the exclamation uttered by the lucky miner who struck gold there in 1850. Gold Mountain was a natural name to choose for this project.

Robin Nelson, the renowned golf course designer with whom we worked in Hawaii, designed a championship golf course. The clubhouse will be Frank Lloyd Wright's unexecuted design for the Nakoma Country Club.

The Garners wanted as many examples of organic architecture as possible, and the first home to be built was Taliesin's 1997 *Life* Dream House. We have designed a series of model homes and have several custom-designed homes underway. Lot sales have exceeded all expectations. Gold Mountain will be an example of building in total harmony with the natural environment. The forest, the mountains, boulders, wildflowers, lakes, and streams—all will be cherished and preserved.

Gold Mountain is planned so as to preserve the natural forest, rivers, and mountains.

INTEGRAL ARTS

What you appreciate, you own. Art is an inner experience, not something you can know; it is something deeper than what you can know. And you have to arrive at it by being.
—FLLW

Heloise Christa at work on a model of "St. Elizabeth Seton".

Great periods in the history of the world are largely defined by the art and architecture that they produced. For the spirit of architecture to continue to flourish, architects must search for ways to renew their creative vitality and energy. For a design to be inspired, the artist must be inspired. At Taliesin we actively work on this aspect, constantly engaging in learning, exploring, and experiencing many different forms of artistic expression.

Architecture is, for us, the mother art. It embraces sculpture, painting, music, dance, drama, and poetry. We participate in all. We design and make murals, art glass windows and screens, and ceramics. We not only build and renovate our buildings at Taliesin and Taliesin West, but we maintain them on a daily basis. Arranging the furniture, setting the dining tables and designing flower arrangements are all forms of artistic expression that give fresh meaning to our work. As we integrate these forms of art into architecture we are integrating our work and our lives. There is, after all, some form of art to everything in life, and new ideas are generated when artists expand their horizons. There is an art to cooking, to farming, to business, to talking, to everything that we do in life.

We design and make cabinets, wood and steel furniture, lighting fixtures, tableware, carpets, and fabrics. We do photography, design costumes and jewelry, and arrange flowers. We make abstract designs, graphic designs, and computer art. There are few forms of art that we have not explored and few media that we have not used to express our art. Every day we seek for ways to integrate art and architecture with life.

*"The Wings of Phoenix"—rebirth
is part of human evolution.*

Our ideas and designs in art and architecture come from nature, they come from life. To connect to the source of ideas we strive to identify the fundamental structure of things. The abstract geometry that underlies nature may be obvious or it may be subtle. It is in the search for it that we begin to perceive how it is organized, to understand what makes it work. We marvel at the seemingly infinite variety of forms, shapes, colors, and textures that can issue from this appreciation.

Wright gave this poetic description of the process: "As we pass along the wayside some blossom with glowing color attracts us. Held by it we gratefully accept its perfect loveliness. Seeking the secret of its ineffable charm, we find the blossom intimately related to the texture and shape of the foliage beneath. We are led on to discover a resultant pattern of structure.

Above: *Eugene Masselink at work*
—art is an inner experience,
deeper than something you can
just know.

Left: *Masselink's mural in cypress*
wood, oils, stain, and gold leaf.

Left: *Frank Lloyd Wright examines Kay Rattenbury's sculpture.*

Below: *"Awakening" by Heloise Christa. Only by awakening can we ascend to a new state of being.*

Right: *Chairs designed by Frank Lloyd Wright, manufactured by Cassina.*

Below: *Gates to the Marin County Civic Center.*

Structure as now we may observe proceeds from generals to particulars arriving at the blossom. We have here a thing organic. We may study with profit these manifest truths of form and structure."

Young apprentices at Taliesin are encouraged to participate in many expressions of art. We have exhibitions of their sculpture and other forms of art from time to time. To see their ideas, as they struggle to bring them to life, and the remarkable variety of creations that they produce, is an inspiration. Each work of art is a challenge to an individual, and there is a synergy that develops as we support and encourage each other in our work.

Artistic sensibilities and creative abilities are enhanced by the appreciation of different art forms. So architecture is influenced by music, sculpture by dance, poetry by drama, painting by photography. All are interconnected.

Our adventures in art are inspired by the myriad patterns of nature. Our passion for our work and our search for new ideas makes the experience profound and everlasting.

Keep your love of nature, for that is the true way to understand art and more.

—Vincent Van Gogh

Above: *Susan Lockhart working on a glass design.*

Right: *Etched glass design.*

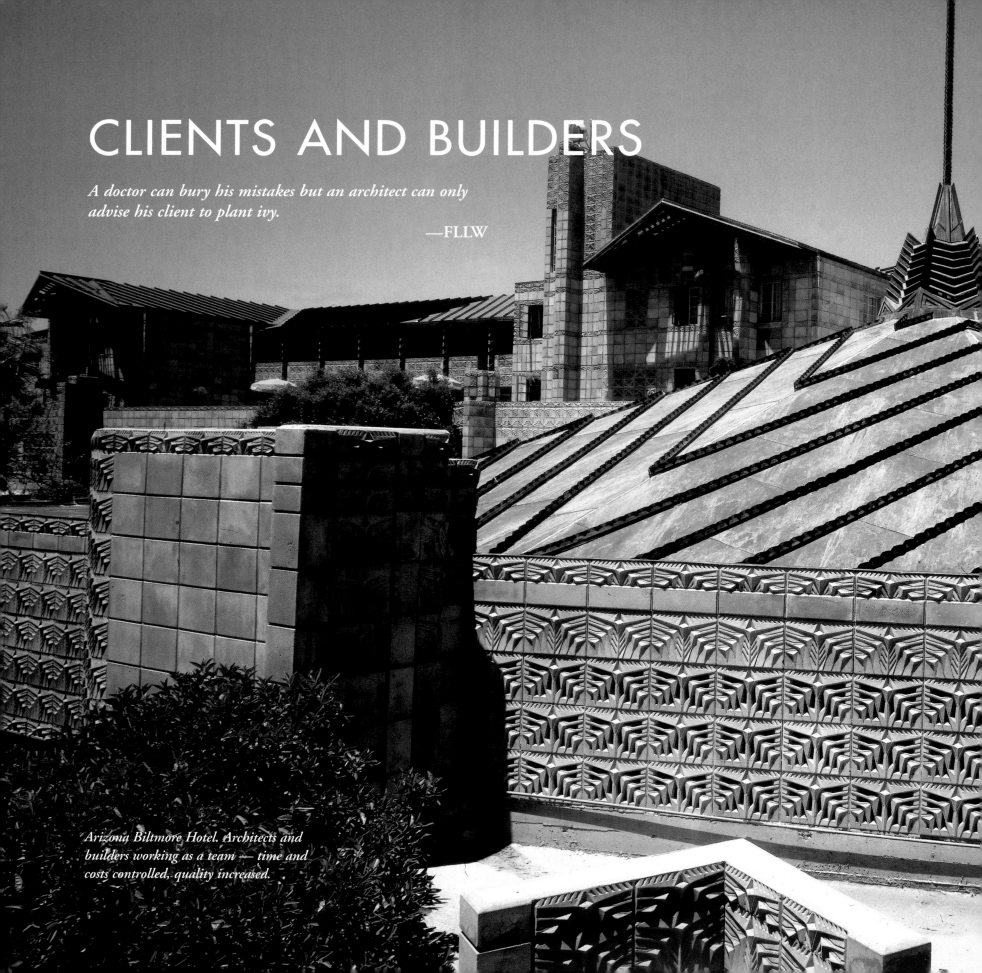

CLIENTS AND BUILDERS

A doctor can bury his mistakes but an architect can only advise his client to plant ivy.

—FLLW

Arizona Biltmore Hotel. Architects and builders working as a team — time and costs controlled, quality increased.

Architecture is an amalgam of science, business, and art. Architects are distinct from other artists in that they depend upon so many other people in order for their work to be accomplished. They need both a client and a builder. Artists can create their work without a client. But until an architect's design is built, it may exist as a beautiful drawing, but it is not architecture.

At Gammage Auditorium, both audience and performers are critics and clients.

Seventh Day Adventist office building roof framing. Good builders like to be challenged.

CLIENTS

Clients play an essential role in the architectural process. A design responds to a client's individual needs, budget, schedule, and site. If the client has a financial partner or investor, there may be another voice in the process. The personal role of clients ranges from very little participation to a great deal. We listen to our clients very carefully. They entrust us with a large investment, often the largest one they ever make. They expect an appropriate return on their venture, not only in financial matters but also in human terms.

A good design brings both tangible and intangible rewards. It is useful, it lasts a long time (with minimal upkeep and repairs), and it appreciates in value. It improves the quality of life and health of the occupants, helps increase productivity, and brings inspiration.

Our goal is to create architecture that is functional and imbued with beauty. It is beauty that nourishes the human spirit. Our relationship with a client often continues long after the building has been completed, and our greatest reward comes when one tells us how much we have added to the quality of their life.

Mr. Wright referred to "His majesty, the client." "No man," said Wright, "can build a building for another who does not believe in him, who does not believe in what he believes in, and who has not chosen him because of this faith, knowing what he can do. That is the nature of architect and client."

While we have a clear responsibility to a client, we have a broader responsibility to society. Not just to society today, but to future generations, since most buildings will be around for a long time. Architecture is the most intimate part of our environment (beyond our clothing, which is ephemeral, and our automobile, also relatively short-lived). Architecture is an art in which everybody is immersed and it has a daily influence on us.

It shapes our lives, shapes our children, shapes the future.

BUILDERS

The urge to build is an innate impulse, one that developed as humankind evolved. There are many builders to be found in nature. Some hereditary instinct guides a bird to build a nest, a beaver to construct a dam, bees to fabricate a honeycomb, and termites to create a citadel. Some creatures, like turtles and mollusks, carry their houses on their backs. Nature-built structures are organic in their use of materials, and beautiful in their integration of form and function.

When primitive humans evolved from living in caves and moved out into the open, they had no genetic factors to rely on to help them know how to build. They had to invent methods of construction. The environment was hostile as were animals and other humans. Thus the most permanent structures were fortresses or places of worship.

A sense of beauty, perhaps first ignited when humans decorated the walls of their caves, began to grow and found expression in buildings. The architectures of ancient civilizations were invariably works of art. The Sumerians, Persians, Egyptians, Chinese, Japanese, Tibetans, and Mayans all developed an organic architecture, appropriate to its time, place, and culture. But gradually, natural ways were replaced by artificial ways. The early Greeks first built columns of bundles of wood sticks. When they learned to carve stone, they fluted their stone columns to imitate the wood bundles. This was the start of classical architecture. When stone was carved to look like wood it was a move away from organic architecture.

The first designs for structures were made by builders and the first architects were constructors. As new materials and methods were devised, the design process was separated from the construction operation. This is unfortunate because the two should always work together. The old, traditional relationship between client, architect, and contractor is poorly structured because it tends to create adversarial relationships. Since the builders, the general contractor, and the subcontractors come onboard after the

The Pearl Palace dome under construction.

design is finished and construction documents are completed, they have little input into the design, engineering, or construction techniques.

A more sensible approach is the design-build method, where everybody is a member of a team who works together as partners. The builder participates in the design phase. From the owner's viewpoint, there is a single-source responsibility for design, cost control, scheduling, construction, and quality assurance.

When you count the number of people involved in an architectural project, from the client to real estate agents, investors, bankers, architects, interior and landscape designers, engineers, consultants, builders, manufacturers, suppliers, governmental agencies, and lawyers, there may be hundreds of participants. Many of them may never know other each other, but all need to work together towards a common objective. When every participant cooperates, when fixing problems is the goal rather than fixing the blame, everybody is a winner. Cooperation, communication, and the coordinated integration of effort are essential to achieving success in architecture.

Organic architecture is the art of building wherein aesthetics and construction not only approve but prove each other.
—FLLW

THE CHALLENGE AHEAD

As for the future, the work shall grow more truly simple; expressive with fewer forms; more articulate with less labor; more fluent, although more coherent; more organic. It shall grow—to fit more perfectly the methods and processes that are called upon to produce it.

—FLLW

Van Wezel Performing Arts Center, Sarasota, Florida. The spirit of architecture will always come from the heart.

For architecture to continue to grow it must eagerly embrace new technology, but never at the expense of humanity and beauty. The center of architecture will always remain the human heart.

Science and industry constantly bring us new materials and methods of construction, but in the application of new and untried materials and methods of construction, architects face a quandary. It takes courage, imagination, and determination to innovate, and the only way to understand the strengths and weaknesses of a new idea is to experiment. But what client is willing to serve as a guinea pig? When a manufacturer produces a new car or airplane, it is the result of much testing and proving of the components, rating their efficiency, and the way they perform together. Architects do not have such resources, so there is a hesitancy to venture forth. This apprehension slows down the growth of architecture. Since life safety is involved, compromise is out of the question, so new construction techniques are slow to develop.

We have taken a small step towards surmounting the problem. At Taliesin West, since we construct the buildings on our campus ourselves, we can experiment with new products and processes. Any successful innovation will advance the cause of architecture and the quality of life; failures will provide us with a learning experience and not harm the public.

Each new project that comes into our studio is an opportunity to create a unique design, unique because it is special to the individual client and special to its particular site. Our passion for our work is fueled by our conviction that our cause is worthy, that we can contribute to the creation of a better world, that we can make a difference. Our eyes are fixed on the future.

THE CITY OF THE FUTURE

Taliesin Architects has been asked to conceive of a model city for the millennium. Working with an entrepreneur, and using Broadacre City as an inspirational source, we are generating ideas for a better urban context. The goal is to create a sustainable city that will provide a more humane environment and better quality of life for its citizens. Building a city requires enormous resources, and this concept is still a vision.

A plan for a new city starts with understanding the successes and failures of past and present urban communities. A new city must be dynamic, allowing for the inexorable law of change. It must be spacious and decentralized, with the family as the basic unit. Democracy, or self-government, where the individual is sovereign, continues to prove itself as the greatest idea for society yet revealed by history.

In their book, *Megatrends 2000,* John Naisbitt and Patricia Aburdene noted: "The great unifying theme

Lincoln Tower, Louisville, Kentucky—building a better future.

*Court of the Seven Seas
—a vision for the future.*

at the conclusion of the 20th century is the triumph of the individual. Threatened by totalitarianism for much of the century, individuals are meeting the millennium more powerfully than before. It is an individual who creates a work of art, embraces a political philosophy, bets a life savings on a new business, inspires a colleague or family member to succeed, emigrates to a new country, has a transcendent spiritual experience. It is an individual who changes him or herself first before attempting to change society. Individuals today can leverage change far more effectively than most institutions. The 1990s are characterized by a new respect for the individual as the foundation of society and the basic unit of change. 'Mass' movements are a misnomer. The environmental movement, the women's movement, the antinuclear movement were all built one consciousness at a time by individuals persuaded of the possibility of a new reality."

Planning the model city will start by locating interested and qualified people who have enthusiasm, experience, determination, and vision. As planning proceeds, we will conduct an international sympo-

sium on city planning. Prominent architects, planners, engineers, environmental scientists, administrators, sociologists, and futurists will be invited to exchange ideas. The process will be one of interaction, moderated by a facilitator who will encourage the group to constructively discuss the many problems of a city. Strengths and weaknesses of cities around the world will be explored in a visioning session. From the synergy of diverse ideas and contradictions a clearer vision of the road ahead will emerge.

Citizens who are subscribers to the idea and want to become residents will recognize the value of living in a beautiful and harmonious environment. The planning process will address long-term goals. Historically, the people of the United States, situated on one of the last continents to be "civilized" and still regarded as the land of opportunity, have been satisfied with a short-term outlook. This attitude of expediency will change as we accept our responsibility to the land and to future generations.

Since it is impossible to reconstruct an existing city, our exemplary city will start from scratch, in the country. It will be strictly limited in both population and size to avoid the over-densification and uncontrolled growth that is common to most cities. Studies indicate that 50,000 residents in a city of 50,000 acres would be ideal. The infrastructure will be carefully planned to be sustainable. Underlying the planning will be a strong guiding philosophy that extends from the inception of planning through development, construction, management, and operation. This city will not be manipulated by vested and special interests, nor be run by a bureaucracy.

What will the new city be like? Uncongested, with clean open spaces, sunlight, green parks, and gardens. A city to nurture rather than assault our senses. Remove the poles and wires, the insolence of signs and advertising, traffic congestion and parking problems, and put in place thoughtful design guidelines, sensibly monitored, and we are half the way towards a city of beauty. Although seeking some of the qualities of James Hilton's "Shangri-La," unlike the utopian community described in his book, *Lost Horizons,* this is not a city that protects the quality of life from erosion through inaccessibility. The new city is open and dynamic, integrated, cosmopolitan, embracing all colors, religious beliefs, age groups, and economic levels.

To as great an extent as possible, the city will be self-sustaining. It will generate much of its own power requirements through alternative energy systems such as photovoltaics. Energy conservation and recycling will be integrated into its fabric. Air and noise pollution will be minimized. Every day the population of our planet increases by two hundred thousand persons. We must find ways to conserve our natural resources.

The city will provide a core area for business and retail merchants. It will have shops and services, hotels, places of worship, education, entertainment and recreation, health care, and a variety of types of single family residences, apartments, and condominiums. It will have light industrial facilities and encompass agriculture, crops, fruits and vegetables, ranches for livestock and poultry. An efficient public transportation system will use clean-fuel vehicles. The scale of the city will encourage walking, jogging, and bicycles.

The city will take full advantage of modern science as an empowerment of the individual. As computers and electronic devices shrink in size and increase in sophistication, they become better tools and impose less on our time and attention. The machinery of technology will help the city run smoothly and efficiently, and will be designed for easy replacement. The infrastructure itself will be built to a higher quality level than the norm for civic standards.

The city will be a healthy place in which to live. Decentralized and humanized, it will provide an environment that promotes the mental, physical, and spiritual well-being of its citizens. The finite size and population will guarantee generous open space, sunlit parks, and green belts within the limits of the city. There will be controls on air quality and noise pollution. It will be a "green" city, environmentally friendly, free and spacious. Efforts will be concentrated on using construction materials and recycled components that do not emit the health-hazardous chemicals commonly found in buildings today. No toxic waste or wasteful landfills. An assured supply of water. Streets configured for safety.

As we seek for the shape of things to come, we see on the horizon exciting new ideas in architecture. We believe that common sense will see that we keep the forces of science and technology in balance with human values.

We have faith that responsible stewardship of our planet will always be a strong and essential part of our conscience. Participation in education will keep us learning; a love of freedom will inspire us to work for democracy. A constant search for beauty will keep our spirits alive and strong. Nature still has many more lessons for us to learn and each day is a new beginning. Our faith lies with the next generation and that faith depends on what each of us does today to build a better future.

The past is but the beginning of a beginning, and all that is and has been is but the twilight of the dawn.
—H.G. Wells

APPENDIX

Index of Projects

*design date

PHOTO CREDITS

page 1: Hedrick Blessing; **p. 2:** Neil Koppes; **p. 4:** Anthony Peres; **p. 10:** Arthur Coleman; **p. 11:** Peres; **p. 12:** Guerrero; **pp. 14, 15, 16, 17:** Taliesin Archives (TA); **pp. 18, 20:** French; **pp. 21, 22, 23, 24:** TA; **p. 26:** Guerrero; **pp. 28, 29:** TA; **p. 30:** Guerrero; **p. 31:** French; **pp. 32, 34:** TA; **p. 34:** Paul Warchol; **p. 35:** TA; **p. 35:** French; **pp. 36, 36:** TA; **p. 37:** Peres; **p. 38:** TA; **pp. 38, 39:** Peres; **pp. 40, 41:** French; **p. 42:** TA; **p. 43:** Peres; **pp. 44 (both), 45:** TA; **p. 47:** Peres; **pp. 48, 49:** Robert Reck; **pp. 50, 51, 52:** TA; **p. 53:** Tony Puttnam; **pp. 54, 55, 56 (both), 57:** TA; **p. 58:** French; **p. 59:** TA; **p. 60:** French; **pp. 60, 61 (both):** TA; **p. 62:** French; **p. 63:** Guerrero; **pp. 63, 64, 65, 66, 67:** TA; **p. 68:** French; **pp. 70, 71, 72, 73:** TA; **p. 74:** Blessing; **pp. 75, 76:** TA; **pp. 77, 78:** French; **pp. 80, 81 (both):** TA; **p. 82:** French; **p. 84:** French; **p. 85:** TA; **p. 86:** Am Players; **pp. 87, 88 (both), 89, 90,. 91, 92:** French; **pp. 93 (both):** TA; **pp. 94, 95, 96:** French; **p. 96:** TA; **pp. 97, 98 (both):** Guerrero; **p. 99:** C. Thomas Hardin; **pp. 100, 101, 102, 103:** TA; **p. 104:** Koppes; **pp. 105, 106, 107 (both):** TA; **p. 108:** Koppes; **p. 109:** TA; **p. 110:** Baltazar Korab; **p. 111:** Koppes; **pp. 112 (both):** TA; **pp. 113, 114, 115 (both):** French; **pp. 116, 117, 118:** Springs Resort; **pp. 119, 120 (both):** Guererro; **p. 121:** TA; **pp. 122 (both), 123 (both):** Guerrero; **p. 124:** French; **p. 125:** TA; **pp. 126, 127 (both), 128:** French; **pp. 129, 130 (both):** TA; **pp. 131, 132, 133 (both):** Guerrero; **pp. 134, 135, 136, 137, 138:** TA; **p. 139:** Marc Bosclair; **p. 140:** TA; **p. 141 (both):** Bosclair; **p. 142, 143:** Reck; **p. 144:** TA; **pp. 144, 145:** Reck; **pp. 146, 147, 148 (both), 149:** TA; **p. 150:** Blessing; **p. 151:** Anderson Ill Assoc.; **pp. 152, 154 (both), 155:** Blessing; **p. 156, 157:** French; **p. 158:** TA; **p. 159:** French; **p. 159:** TA; **pp. 160 (both), 161:** French; **pp. 162, 163, 164 (both), 165:** TA; **p. 166:** French; **pp. 167, 168, 169, 170 (both), 171, 172, 173, 174, 175:** TA; **pp. 176, 177, 178:** French; **pp. 179, 180 (both):** Kalec; **p. 181:** TA; **p. 182:** Reck; **pp. 183, 184, 185, 186 (both), 187:** TA; **pp. 188 (both), 189 (both), 190:** Reck; **pp. 191, 192 (both), 193, 194, 195 (both), 196 (both):** TA; **pp. 197, 198, 199 (both):** French; **pp. 200, 201 (both):** TA; **pp. 202, 203 (both):** Ray Albright; **p. 204:** Peres; **pp. 205, 206, 207 (both), 208 (both), 209:** TA; **pp. 210, 211, 212, 214:** Guerrero; **pp. 215, 216 (both), 217 (both), 218, 219, 220 (both), 221, 222, 223 (both):** TA; **pp. 224, 225, 226 (both), 227 (both):** Peres; **pp. 228, 229, 230 (both), 231, 232, 233, 234 (both):** French; **pp. 235, 236 (both), 237:** Mark Bosclair; **pp. 238, 239:** Arthur Coleman; **p. 240:** TA; **pp. 240, 241:** Coleman; **p. 242:** TA; **pp. 242, 243:** Coleman; **pp. 244, 245, 246 (both), 247:** TA; **p. 247:** French; **pp. 248, 249, 250:** Tim Street-Porter; **pp. 251 (both), 252 (both), 253:** TA; **p. 253:** Wayne Source; **p. 254:** Peres; **pp. 255, 256 (both), 257 (both):** TA; **pp. 258, 259:** Peres; **pp. 260, 261, 262, 263 (both), 264, 265, 266 (both), 267, 268 (both), 269 (both), 270, 271 (both), 272 (both), 273 (both), 274, 275 (both):** TA; **p. 276:** Joann Dost; **pp. 277, 278:** TA; **pp. 278, 279:** Dost; **pp. 280, 281:** French; **pp. 282 (both), 283:** TA; **p. 283:** French; **p. 284 (both):** TA; **p. 285 (both):** French; **p. 286:** TA; **p. 287:** French; **pp. 288, 289, 290:** TA; **p. 291:** Guerrero; **p. 292:** TA.

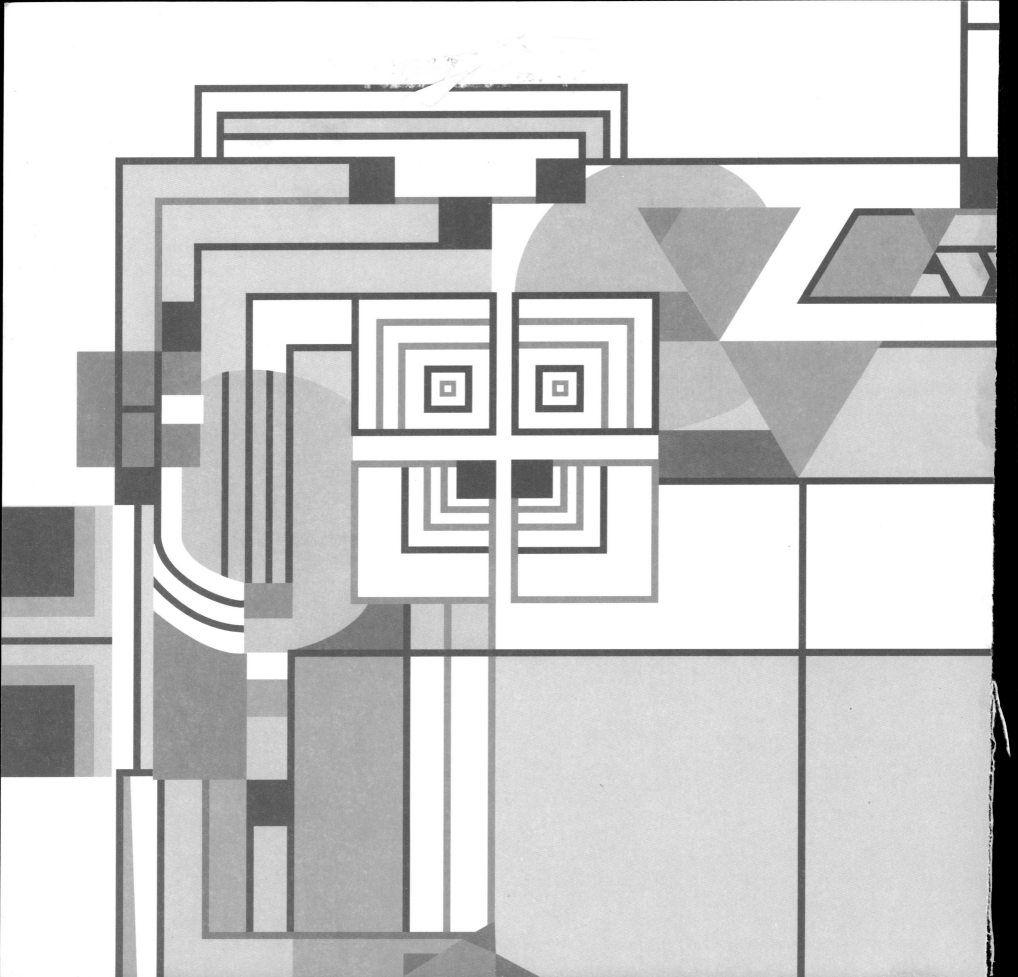